D0522060

God and Caesar

To Dick

without whose love and understanding
this might never have appeared

God and Caesar

Personal Reflections on Politics and Religion

SHIRLEY WILLIAMS

continuum
LONDON • NEW YORK

CONTINUUM
The Tower Building, 11 York Road, London, SE1 7NX
370 Lexington Avenue, New York, NY 10017–6503

www.continuumbooks.com

First published 2003

British Library Cataloguing in Publication Data
A catalogue record for this book is available from the British Library.

ISBN 0 8264 6734 2

Extract from 'Do Not Go Gentle into that Good Night' by Dylan Thomas
reproduced with permission of J. M. Dent.
Extracts from 'Going, going' from *Collected Poems* by Philip Larkin, and
'The History of Truth' and 'The Age of Anxiety' from *Collected Poems* by
W. H. Auden reproduced with permission of Faber and Faber.

Typeset by BookEns Ltd, Royston, Herts.
Printed and bound in Great Britain by MPG Books Ltd,
Bodmin, Cornwall

Contents

Preface

This book is based on a series of lectures I gave at the University of Notre Dame in South Bend, Indiana, under the title *God and Caesar: The Christian in the Modern World*. The first lecture was due to be delivered on 11 September 2001, the day of the terrorist attack on New York and Washington, a day that shattered America's sense of invulnerability with huge consequences for itself and for the rest of the world.

The University of Notre Dame astonished me. On the day after the dreadful event, with its abiding images of violent destruction none of us will forget, the university held a Requiem Mass for the dead. On the next day the students held an open meeting, at which several of the faculty and I spoke, about what would be the morally right, considered response to this atrocity. The language was restrained, the spirit that of trying to understand why other men and women should engage in such an act of hatred against the United States.

I learned from that Mass and that meeting that no one should identify the United States with a crude and united determination to seek retribution and revenge. In this multifarious and self-questioning nation, responses to evil in the world, and indeed in the United States itself, reflect a wide range of principles and values.

Preface

I do not usually find the preparation of lectures daunting. I have given over the years scores of lectures in the Kennedy School of Government at Harvard and indeed elsewhere at home and abroad. But I found presenting the Erasmus lectures both exciting and intimidating. I was very conscious that I was neither a theologian nor a scholar. There were, and are, huge gaps in my knowledge of the Roman Catholic Church, its teachings and its history.

But I was also aware that the Church needed, badly, to hear the voices of the laity, not least the women in the laity, who for so long have been expected to be obedient, pious and silent. I knew too that the Church, and indeed more widely the mainstream Christian churches, had to contend with modernization and globalization, and that many of the traditional responses would no longer suffice.

Of course I recognized my own inadequacies. So I brought together a small group of Catholic friends, men and women who not only shared my concerns but had done everything they could to address them. We spent an intensive weekend at my house in the Hertfordshire countryside discussing each of the lectures. Those friends, like friends in other spheres of my life, enriched my understanding with their comments and criticisms.

I wish I could respond as Edward Elgar did in the *Enigma Variations*, by describing each of them in inspired music. I cannot. In words, they are John Wilkins, the perceptive, wise and merciful editor of *The Tablet*, one of the few journals I read all through almost every week; Lavinia Byrne, who brings a surpassing gift for communication to her dissemination of the word of God, enthusing thousands of people who have lost touch with the Church, yet who was curbed and censured by the Vatican for daring to raise the issue of women's ordination; and Father John Feighery, now a priest in Dublin, a missionary of the Divine Word and a man of sensibility and intellectual brilliance. He showed me, in the teeming barrios of Brazil, how the spirit of Christ moves among the poorest and most desperate of God's people. That experience is recounted in the chapter of this book called 'The Gospel to the Poor'.

In these chapters I have tried to explore the relationship between Christian teaching, the Christian churches and public life in the modern world. Some of the things I write about are relevant to all religions, namely the spiritual and moral dimensions of public life. For I have found that public life presents one with a series of moral conflicts and moral dilemmas, some of them extremely difficult to resolve. Some are particularly relevant to Christians, for whom the life of Jesus Christ on this earth provides powerful guidance. Some specifically engage Catholic Christians, whose clerics have for centuries not hesitated to proclaim its doctrines and counsel those in public life about how to behave.

What right have I to talk about such matters, for I am neither a moral philosopher nor a theologian? Only the authority of experience. I have fought ten General Elections and two by-elections in the United Kingdom. In some of these I won, in some I lost, in equal proportions. In addition, I campaigned nationally in three other elections.

As an elected politician, I was a member of the House of Commons in the United Kingdom for sixteen years. For four of these years, I was a junior departmental minister in ministries concerned with labour, education and science and home affairs. For nearly five more, I was a member of the Cabinet, first in an economic department concerned with prices and consumer affairs, then as Secretary of State for Education and Science and Paymaster General. In between, I was for four years official spokesperson for the Opposition on subjects ranging from prisons to social security. I co-founded a new political party, the Social Democratic Party, in 1981, and was re-elected to Parliament for my new party for a further year. I helped to bring about its merger with the Liberal Party, and am today leader of that merged party, the Liberal Democrats, in the United Kingdom's upper house, the House of Lords.

As a Catholic politician, I have been active in certain Catholic organizations. I am a vice-president of CAFOD, the Catholic Fund for Overseas Development. I was one of the keynote speakers at the national conference organized by the Archbishop of Liverpool in 1999 on 'Catholics in Public Life'. I have worked closely with bishops and members of the clergy on the plight of refugees and asylum-seekers. In Great Britain, the Roman Catholic and Anglican Churches have joined forces to press for merciful and generous treatment of those fleeing persecution and torture.

Secondly, on the academic side, I was for twelve years Public Service Professor of Elective Politics, first full-time, then part-time and now emeritus, at the John F. Kennedy School of Government at Harvard University. The qualification for such a professorship is to have thought and written about public life while being actively engaged in it. It is an exciting, sometimes controversial, attempt to bridge the gulf between the world of action and the world of ideas. And, not least illuminating for me, I have taught and worked over the years in India, Russia, Eastern Europe and South and West Africa, the latter four during critical years of transition to democracy.

I have spent most of my life among colleagues, both in politics and in academia, with no strong commitment to Christianity. I assume that, as far as politics is concerned, such a situation would not be typical of American Christians, who would find themselves among believers, albeit that those believers might well disagree strongly among themselves on matters of foreign and domestic policy, and on the interpretation of the relevant lessons from the Scriptures. In academic life, the prevailing attitude of my colleagues on both sides of the Atlantic has been one of scepticism towards religious belief tempered with tolerance and sometimes curiosity. That itself is very different from the intense sectarianism of the nineteenth and early twentieth centuries, when my father, a young English convert to Roman Catholicism and the son of an Anglican vicar, could not decide whether it was safer to walk down an 'orange' or a 'green' street in Liverpool, the city of his birth. Such bitter sectarianism in the United Kingdom today survives only in Northern Ireland and a few parts of Scotland, doing immense damage to the public perception of Christianity in practice.

Arthur Schlesinger Junior's characterization of the American Mind, in his brilliant denunciation of absolutism, as 'by nature and tradition skeptical, irreverent, pluralistic and relativistic',[1] sounded to me like an excellent description of the mind, not so much of all Americans, as of the intellectuals and pragmatists I have known as colleagues, whether in the United States or in Britain. It sounded unlike the Americans I had met over the years in Alabama, the Appalachians, Wyoming and the Midwest, men and women of strong and sometimes dogmatic faith. But then intellectuals and the 'serious' media with whom they associate are not usually typical of their fellow-citizens.

NOTE

1. Arthur Schlesinger Jr, address at the inauguration of Vartan Gregorian as President of Brown University, printed in *The New York Times Book Review*, 23 July 1989.

Introduction

I am often asked in Catholic circles whether I am a cradle Catholic or a convert, to which the only honest answer is that I am both. My mother, the writer Vera Brittain, was brought up as a traditional middle-class Anglican, but harboured considerable doubts about the practice of her Church. In particular, she had been repelled during the First World War by its uncritical patriotism.

My father, born in Liverpool and the son of an Anglican vicar, was a convert to Roman Catholicism. He had no previous connections with that Church. His conversion was an intellectual one, based on his reading of the works of Cardinal Newman, and subsequently of the Church Fathers, in particular the *Summa Theologica* of St Thomas Aquinas. As I grew up, my father extolled to me the wisdom of the Church Fathers. Believing, like James Mill, the father of John Stuart Mill, that even infants could grasp complicated ideas, he would read extracts from the *Summa* to me when I was only four or five, carefully explaining the meaning of the texts. That was the sense in which I was, almost literally, a 'cradle Catholic'.

My parents were progressive thinkers, and agreed that

1

their children, my older brother John and me, should not be baptized into either the Roman Catholic Church or the Church of England, but should be free to choose when they became adult. My early childhood coincided with my father's angry breach with the Church of Rome. In 1937, he had visited Spain to see for himself the plight of refugees from the bitter civil war in that country, between forces loyal to the government and the armies of General Francisco Franco. My father's democratic and socialist convictions meant that he supported the elected Spanish government, and in this he was reinforced by the commitment to it of many of the parish priests he met in Barcelona and other Catalonian towns. He was therefore outraged by the close relationship between the Catholic Church of Spain and General Franco, and lapsed from the practice of his faith.

I was a small child at the time of these stirring political events. But my soul was not to be put in jeopardy because of them. My parents' young housekeeper, Amy Burnett, was a devout Catholic. She and her husband Charles, a Catholic from Newcastle, took me to church every Sunday. They were convinced that 'the professor', as they called my father, would someday return to the Church, and they were right. Compelled to consider 'the last things' by some hours in an open lifeboat after his ship had been torpedoed in the Atlantic in December 1941, he resumed the practice of his religion.

Two aspects of Roman Catholicism had always attracted him, its willingness to engage in intellectual argument, and its theatricality. He loved the ceremonial, the liturgy and the history. He loved Latin, a language he knew well, and he cherished the great Tridentine Mass. I am not sure if the conclusions of Vatican II on the liturgy and the use of indigenous languages appealed to him.

In 1950, my father and I went to Rome together to celebrate the Holy Year. The great church of St Peter was ablaze with candles, and one could feel it emerging from the darkness of the war years and of the Nazi period before that. We had a private audience with the Pope, Pius XII. Refined and frail, he seemed almost translucent in his gold and white vestments. At that time, before controversy bruised his reputation, he appeared almost saint-like, removed in his spirituality from the horrors of the secular world. My father and I visited together the other great churches of Rome, among them Santa Maria Maggiore, and my father's favourite, St John Lateran. He knew the histories of each one.

My mother's influence on me was as great as my father's. If he made me a Catholic, she made me a Christian, for I was uneasy with the pomp and remoteness of my father's Church at that time. My mother's deepest sympathies were evoked by the dissenters, men and women inspired by conscience rather than by institutional loyalties. Her model was John Bunyan, the author of *The Pilgrim's Progress*.

I spent a week with her in Bedfordshire in the winter of 1948, where she was researching a biography of him. We visited together the towns and villages where he had preached, Ampthill, Elstow, Bedford itself, and identified the landmarks which were transformed in *Pilgrim's Progress* into the Slough of Despond and the Delectable Mountains. It was not entirely devotion to my mother that brought me to Bedfordshire, however. I had fallen in love with Peter Parker, then a celebrity at Oxford, the university we both attended, and later Chairman of British Rail. Knowing he lived in Bedford, I hoped to catch some glimpse of him among the monuments to the town's greatest forefather.

My mother's natural allies were the Quakers, whose meetings she sometimes attended. I asked her once why she had, in the end, remained an Anglican rather than joining the Society of Friends, with whom she had so much in common, not least pacifism. She replied that the Quakers were too good for her. The Church of England was a church of sinners, and, as a sinner too, that was where she belonged.

It was possible for her to remain an Anglican only because the Church of England covered such a wide spectrum of values and attitudes. In her day that ranged from the unbending conservatism of Cosmo Gordon Lang to the informed compassion of William Temple and George Bell, from the angry patriotism of Dean Inge to the visionary pacifism of Dick Sheppard.

But if I was a cradle Catholic, I was also a convert. My parents' marriage was based on recognition of each other's autonomy and each other's convictions, though in practice my mother's professional priorities usually determined our domestic arrangements. So, as they had agreed, I did not seek to be baptized until I went to Oxford in October 1948. I arranged to be baptized at St Aloysius, the rather gloomy church that stands next to my college, Somerville.

It was not an auspicious occasion. One or two friends came to the church, but they were not Catholics, so I summoned a helpful stranger in the church to be my godmother. She was clearly a devout and responsible woman. She paid an unheralded visit to my college room the next day, and was shocked to see me in trousers, dispensing toast and coffee to friends of both sexes sitting on the floor. I think it must have been the trousers that really upset her, because she did not try to make contact again.

At Oxford I went occasionally to the Newman Society but was never part of the exclusive Catholic groups, usually young men and women from distinguished recusant families. Indeed, I did not care for the often snobbish and inward-looking atmosphere in these groups. My friends came from all religious backgrounds and from none. Among my closest friends, a high proportion were, and are, Jewish.

My religious views were not particularly well formed despite my father's efforts. I had never attended a Catholic school, and my hold on the catechism and the lives of the saints was uncertain. My belief in God was rooted in an almost pantheistic love of His creation. From infancy, I felt rapture at the natural world. My earliest words, according to my father, were inspired by the garden of our Chelsea terraced house on a summer's day. 'Isn't it ni!' I announced.

As I grew up among the lakes and forests of wartime Minnesota, and later, back in England, in the New Forest and the fells of Westmorland where my great-uncle and aunt lived, I asked myself how could anything so ravishingly, so simultaneously awesome and delicately beautiful as the natural world, have come into being other than through the genius of an all-knowing, loving and omnipotent God? Among the protagonists of the Argument from Design, I was certainly one.

This celebration of nature was confirmed by an early acquaintance with poetry. My father presented me each birthday with a new edition of one of the modern poets who emerged in the 1930s, T. S. Eliot, Wystan Hugh Auden, Robert Frost and many more. I still possess an early edition of the *Four Quartets*, inscribed by my father to 'Poppy, my Ugly, on her second birthday'. My mother had written poems as a VAD (Voluntary Aid Detachment) nurse, and later while she was at Oxford, mainly recollecting her experiences in the First World War.

More influential than these was my introduction to poetry by two outstanding teachers at St Paul's Girls' School which I attended from 1943 to 1947, apart from a year when I was evacuated to Bournemouth. Rosamund Jenkinson and Margaret Higginson were immersed in great poetry. They inspired their lumpish and grumpy pupils. To this day, lines of poetry come into my head. The metaphysical poets, Thomas Traherne, Richard Jefferies, Henry Vaughan, together with William Wordsworth and William Blake, were the high priests of my faith. For me, the corn in the August fields was always 'orient and immortal wheat'.

None of this was a reason to be a Catholic. Of course I was influenced by my father and by Amy and Charles Burnett. I felt at one with the internationalism of Roman Catholics, so much at odds with the national ethos at that time of the Church of England. But I think the main reason I chose to be and remain a Catholic lay in the claims the Church made for herself, and in the demands she made on her adherents. 'I am the Way, the Truth and the Life'; 'You are Peter, and on this rock I shall build my church, and the gates of Hell shall not prevail against it.' These are breathtaking claims. It seemed to me that, if I was to be a Christian, I should embrace Christianity in its strongest form. It was the huge claims and the huge demands made that drew me to the Church of Rome.

THE MODERN WORLD

I like a lot of things about the modern world, its eclecticism, its fantastic range of choice, the ease of movement across borders. I like modern Britain with its colour and diversity much better than the class-ridden, stilted country in which I grew up. The explosion of enthusiasm for music, popular and classical alike, for art, both modern and traditional, for the theatre and the opera bear witness to an exciting, lively country.

But I have one lament for the past that grows deeper with every passing year. It is a lament for the natural world, for God's creation, whose beauty and magic was the foundation of my early faith. Philip Larkin, a sour poet but a man with an acute sense of beauty, wrote the epitaph of England's countryside:

> *Going, going*
> I thought it would last my time –
> The sense that, beyond the town,
> There would always be fields and farms,
> Where the village louts could climb
> Such trees as were not cut down
>
> [...]
>
> It seems just now,
> To be happening so very fast;
> Despite all the land left free
> For the first time I feel somehow
> That it isn't going to last
>
> [...]
>
> And that will be England gone,
> The shadows, the meadows, the lanes,
> The guildhalls, the carved choirs.
> There'll be books; it will linger on
> In galleries; but all that remains
> For us will be concrete and tyres.
>
> *Philip Larkin,* Collected Poems
> The Marvell Press – Faber & Faber (1988)

England in my childhood was a land of hidden places, of hedges and copses, of secret gardens behind wooden doors, of woods protecting mists of bluebells. My favourite childhood book was called *Perkin the Peddler*, by Eleanor Farjeon. I have it still. It is a book about the names of villages, and the stories behind their names – Appledore, Blowers Green, Chipping Norton and, strangest of all, Yeavering Bell. I was enchanted by the stories and the woodcut illustrations that went with them.

Most of these villages and small towns today will have nicely painted cottages, gardens neatly planted, the bushes tidy and a shiny car by the curb or in the garage. As places to live, they will be pleasanter and more convenient than they used to be, rural suburbs rather than traditional villages. But there will be no magic of discovery, no crannies to explore. Furthermore, that secret world is now fenced off because responsible parents are constantly watchful for their children, fearing crime, abduction or accidents. They take the children to and from school by car. There is no chance to explore the wild flowers or the berries in the hedges.

Many people persuade themselves that predators on children are a new phenomenon. But that is not true. Read Charles Dickens and other Victorian novelists on the exploitation of children for almost all purposes. Recognize how widespread incest used to be, in rural cottages and congested urban houses, for decades a crime against children few adults were prepared to admit existed.

In my own childhood, which because of the war was not a sheltered one, I often encountered such predators. As a young girl of thirteen, I was confronted by a group of sailors intent on raping my best friend and me on the ship on which we returned to England from three years' evacuation in the United States. We escaped into the gentleman's lavatory and from there into one of the lifeboats on deck. At fourteen, evacuated again from my London school to Bournemouth, I used to cycle home for the weekend to my parents' cottage in the New Forest. More than once I came across men who exposed themselves, though I could never understand why they imagined chilly penises were attractive. My parents were unaware of these occasions, and I never told them. But I was grateful to them for not trying to suppress my sense of adventure.

Even in the countryside nowadays, children's sense of exploration, of awe at the natural world, is stifled. Much of the farmland has become lifeless and sterile, hedges rooted out, the birds and butterflies gone, the footpaths choked by brambles and nettles because they are no longer much used.

The natural world now is less a constant presence than a theme park, well designed undoubtedly, but devoid of the adventure and enchantment that gave many children a sense of the presence of the Creator. 'Surprised by joy', that wonderful phrase from Wordsworth's *Desideria*, captures those emotions – the bright yellow of lime trees and the silver of aspen in an autumn landscape, the wind patterns on water, the high clouds building up in the summer sky. We do not have much time now even to see such things, and television brings us much more sensational images of natural phenomena. But somewhere, the mystery of discovery, the God of small things, the Holy Spirit moving among us, slips unnoticed away.

THE DEATH OF DEFERENCE

My predecessor as MP for East Hertfordshire, Sir Derek Walker-Smith, part of whose constituency I inherited, used to pay rather grand visits from time to time to his respectful electors. There would be a programme in the local newspaper of his progress across the constituency. Older men would touch their caps briefly when they met him. After all, he was a Member of Parliament, a man of influence and position.

The last remains of feudalism could still be found in cottages on great estates in the 1960s. More than one elector during the General Election campaign of 1964 asked me to speak to him behind the sweet peas and the hollyhocks, so that our conversation could not be observed. Others asked me if the ballot really was secret. And on many doorsteps, the woman of the house would shout down the passage, 'What are we, George (or Bert or John)? Are we Labour?'

Deference to elders and betters ranged far beyond politics. Priests wore black soutanes down to their ankles, and nuns were encased in habits from head to toe. The clergy looked like clergy, and were generally respected. Well-off women demonstrated their wealth in furs and expensive jewellery. No parent ever encountered a headmistress in trousers, or a headmaster in a casual sweater. Position was visible in clothes, accents, even body language.

The modern world, however, is unimpressed by position. Men and women have to live up to the standards they claim to live by. The clergy, like others in positions of authority, may be respected for their dedication and compassion; they will not be respected for wearing dog collars and black suits.

I had the good fortune to know as friends some wonderful priests, men who tried to follow the example of Jesus Christ and to serve His Church for all its flaws. When I was an undergraduate, I got to know a young Italian priest, Giancarlo Colombo, who had been sent to study philosophy at Oxford. He and my first husband Bernard, who was to become one of the world's leading philosophers, became great friends, though even Giancarlo failed to convert Bernard to Catholicism.

Giancarlo's parents must have loved the paintings of El Greco, for their son's long, gaunt, elegant face and dark brown eyes came straight from the portraits of that great master. He was a man of the deepest faith, intent on exploring the reason for his beliefs as far as that could take him. He loved human beings, and rejoiced in their happiness. He had chosen celibacy as his gift to God, but it was not easy for him. He once said to us, 'If I had not been a priest, I could have found a world in women.'

Before he went back to his community in Bormio in the Italian Alps, not far from where my mother's beloved brother Edward had been killed in the last months of the First World War, Giancarlo asked Bernard and me if we would travel part of the way with him, first to Bruges, which he longed to see, and then across Switzerland. Giancarlo was a Jesuit, and Jesuits were not at that time allowed into Switzerland, so he had to travel in ordinary clothes, shorn of any clerical garb. The three of us stayed in small bed-and-breakfast farmhouses without booking ahead of time. Yet, in each Swiss village, when Giancarlo walked down to the local church to say his daily morning Mass, villagers appeared from nowhere to worship alongside him.

When we finally left him, instead of the usual goodbye and promise to meet soon, Giancarlo blessed us and told us how much our friendship meant to him, and intimated that we might not see one another again. His farewell proved prophetic. A few months later, carrying a crucifix up a mountain ridge to a climbers' Mass, Giancarlo slipped and fell into the abyss below. His superior wrote of him that he was one of the finest priests he had ever known.

There have been other priests I have admired and loved. One of them is Father Feighery, who has become my family's unofficial chaplain, and who was one of the four friends I consulted about this book. He is the priest about whom I write in Chapter 5, 'The Gospel to the Poor', who served as a missionary in Brazil for fourteen years. I got to know him through correspondence. Over the years my life has been so burdened with letters, dozens every week, that I can barely bring myself to encourage protracted corres-pondence. But Father John's first letter from Brazil, about something I had said publicly, was so perceptive, had such insight into politics, that I found myself reading every word. For several years, until I visited Brazil in 1984, we corresponded but never met. He is the kind of priest the Church most needs.

In South Africa in 1990, and again in 1994, I met many men and women who lived the Gospels, nonconformists, Anglicans and Catholics alike. The great African contributions to Christianity are joy and forgiveness. I shall not forget Archbishop Tutu, then Chancellor of the University of the Western Cape, dancing across the platform to hug a distinguished lady who was receiving an honorary degree, and then dancing back with her. Such expressions of joy are rare indeed among the po-faced English clergy, though things may be changing for the better.

As for forgiveness, my husband Dick and I felt humble encountering the generosity of spirit we met in South Africa. There was the man in the Pretoria township of Mamelodi who had spent seven years in jail for distributing pamphlets, and, one week after his release, invited us to lunch in his house, at which he pleaded with many militant youngsters for reconciliation with their white oppressors. There was the Afrikaaner minister who himself lived in an African township, and had the courage to denounce the atrocities perpetrated against Africans by his own community. And there was the little middle-aged priest I met in Durban, who had stood before his church door in his underpants in the middle of the night, telling a Zulu posse that they would have to kill him before he would allow them into the church where some 60 terrified Xhosas were hiding.

Each of these men and women renew our faith, as do the great martyrs and saints of the past, such as Dietrich Bonhoeffer, Archbishop Romero and Bishop Hélder Câmara of Recife. The Church is not always quick to recognize them. To me, Archbishop Romero died for his faith as did

Thomas Becket, but the cause for his canonization moves slowly, compared to the more ambiguous figure of Pope Pius XII. As for Hélder Câmara, a saint in the eyes of his desperately poor people, and deservedly so, there is no official recognition of his life of service and love. Once I saw him in the packed and dark cathedral of São Paulo. As he preached, his tiny figure seemed suffused with light. The power of his words lifted him above the huge congregation.

It is the witness of these great Christians that makes the charges against the clergy of paedophilia and of harbouring paedophiles so heartbreaking. Paedophilia is the most loathed of crimes, because it steals a child's innocence. Paedophilia among the clergy twists every virtue once associated with the priesthood: trustworthiness, goodness, mercy, compassion, purity. The Roman Catholic clergy has in most modern Christian countries been respected, even held up for admiration by non-Catholics. That is one reason why the charges against priests, in some cases borne out by the evidence, are so damaging.

Just as serious for the Church are the attempts by bishops to deal with accused priests by moving them to other parishes or out of parochial work altogether. Our Western societies today are suspicious of any attempt at evasion or conceal-ment. It arouses immediate suspicion, and that suspicion in turn attracts the bloodhounds of the media.

The Church's tradition has long been to deal with its problems in-house, and to close the doors against the intrusions of outsiders. Some of the problems have been swept under the carpet. That is how the Church has dealt with the widespread disregard of its teachings on contra-ception and homosexuality. Many bishops have acted in that familiar way. But trying to deal with accusations of clerical paedophilia by evasion or concealment will be lethal – I use the word carefully – for the Church.

What is so sad is that the majority of innocent priests and religious have been scarred by the offences of a small minority. Parents will be less open, reluctant to trust priests with their children. People confessing their sins will ask themselves if the man behind the grille is not more sinful than they are. The crisis confronting the Church on this issue could not be more serious.

Up to now, the Church's response has been great harshness towards guilty priests, inquiries headed by respected lay figures, former judges being especially favoured, and more careful examination of seminarians. But it will not do. The crisis goes down to the very heart of the Church, and can only be dealt with by a root-and-branch reform of the priesthood.

ENTER EVE

Why? Because of two phenomena not well understood by a hierarchy distant from the ways of the modern world. These are first, the women's revolution, whose impact on the Church I attempt to describe in my third chapter, 'Enter Eve'. Women have emerged from that revolution as autonomous and intelligent beings, capable of matching men intellectually and professionally. That means the possibility of marriage as a partnership of friends and equals, a satisfying response to human loneliness as well as offering the traditional blessing of children.

Second is the removal of almost all the social inhibitions associated with sex. Television programmes endlessly address the topic. Advertisements are constructed around sexual arousal and sexual innuendo. Families today talk easily about sexuality and sexual orientation. The young man or woman who has opted for celibacy can have little idea of the temptations he or she will have to resist.

That is why the scapegoating of pathetic priestly paedophiles is so cruel. Caught between his or her vows and a society clamorous with sex, no longer inhibited as were the societies of their grandparents, many young priests and religious must despair. Added to that is the loneliness of being a priest on one's own, the cold priests' houses and the too often unsympathetic and grumpy housekeepers, chosen precisely because they offer no temptation to anyone.

The Church must now examine the rule of celibacy, the refusal to accept married clergy and the refusal even to consider the ordination of women. As to married clergy, the Vatican's acceptance of Anglican priests, who were invited to continue their sacerdotal duties and were not required to become celibate if already married, surely drives a coach and horses through the Vatican's defences.

Women's liberation crops up frequently in the pages of this book. The Church has assumed the obedience to it of women for a long time and has on the whole been justified in that assumption. Women still constitute the majority of lay members. Most of them have accepted the model of the Virgin Mary, loving and caring for their families and accepting the part in life God has given them.

As evidence mounts, however, that women are as intelligent as men, as capable of leadership, as courageous, the role the Church accords them is no longer adequate. Women look at the world the leadership of men has given them and see poverty, cruelty, conflict and despair. In country after country, from Chile to Ireland, women demonstrate against these evils. Some of the few who acquire power embrace the rules of the political game but others resist. Among the resisters are some outstanding Catholic women: Mary Robinson, Corazon Aquino, Barbara Ward, to mention only three.

In spite of the evidence, the hierarchy continues to treat

women in public life with indifference or contempt. It took a fierce campaign to get the United Nations organization to appoint women to senior positions as heads of agencies or as Deputy Secretary. No such campaign has got anywhere near persuading the Church to appoint women to non-sacerdotal positions in the Church hierarchy. Yet, on issues such as celibacy and paedophilia, the Church needs, more than it realizes, the advice of women as well as of men.

'Anatomy is destiny,' said Freud. That is no longer self-evident, given the scientific advances since the 1960s, in particular the contraceptive pill. Easy and cheap contraception ushered women into a new world of freedom. The Church saw birth control as a licence for immorality, and of course it could be. But for millions of married women contraception meant liberation from the burden of repeated pregnancies, and an end to the misery of abortion as the one way to deal with unwanted births. The Church has never faced up to the fact that abortion is widely practised in Catholic countries.

My personal belief is that the Church's opposition to contraception, which of course does not involve the destruction of potential human life, severely undermined its crusade against abortion. As a young MP, I opposed David Steel's private bill to legalize abortion. I still regard abortion as wrong, and late or partial birth abortion as abhorrent, involving as it does the deliberate destruction of a viable human being. But I was convinced that the bill's opponents had little chance of stopping the bill from becoming law if they also opposed birth control. That was a view shared by many Anglicans too.

The Church offered its own solution, which was celibacy. But celibacy is a huge strain on marriage, and may have to extend over many years if there are medical or economic reasons for limiting the size of the family. Having gone through four miscarriages in four years, I can bear testimony to the difficulty of adhering to the Church's teaching, a difficulty celibate men cannot begin to understand. Preaching celibacy is wholly unrealistic. In patriarchal societies, the men decide what happens, and the women are expected to obey, regardless of consequences.

The Church has found it very difficult to talk about sexual matters. Because it lacks the support of the laity, it has compromised on the basis of mutual hypocrisy as far as birth control is concerned. The faithful see nothing to confess, and many priests nothing to condemn. This is not something that can be left to time to resolve. Hypocrisy corrupts the Church. It would be helpful for the next Pope to convene a new commission of lay men and women as well as clergy, like the one that advised Paul VI on *Humanae Vitae* and was so unhappily overridden. Without an understanding of the new forces in society, and a considered response to them, the Church will become irrelevant to many of its people. In a world as beset by evil as ours, that would be a tragedy.

THE FOUR HORSEMEN

Beset by evil. 'The Four Horsemen of the Apocalypse', whose ravages I address in my seventh chapter, seemed for a time to be curbed. Somehow the world avoided nuclear war, and stepped back from the brink of destruction during the Cuban missile crisis. The Cold War antagonists moved into a long period of hibernation after the Vietnam War, fighting their battles through surrogates in Asia and Africa. The hopeful political and economic development of these countries was in consequence negated, but threatened no peace except their own.

Democracy, as the Nobel laureate economist Amartya

Sen has explained, held governments accountable for famine, and famines no longer occur in democratic countries. Public health and immunization vanquished certain serious diseases like smallpox, and turned others, like tuberculosis, from scourges into rarities. The world held the technical means to eliminate them in its hands.

The other great force for good in those post-war decades was the growing reliance on political solutions instead of war. The outstanding example is the European Union, to whose construction I have devoted much of my political life. Blasé as Europeans are, most of us simply fail to recognize the scale of that achievement. Yes, it is tiresomely bureaucratic, complicated, deficient in democratic accountability. But in the scales of history, none of those factors begins to outweigh its three great accomplishments, the end of war in the entire European continent, the creation of a common regime of European law based on human rights and the achievement of a single market of 350 million people.

Europe has also become the pioneer of an international system that transcends the nation state, rather like the Holy Roman Empire in pre-Westphalian times, an international system that subscribes to certain common standards and values, including rules of behaviour like those embodied in the Geneva Conventions, and in United Nations' treaties and conventions on weapons of mass destruction.

Only a few short years ago, building that initial structure into a global rule of law did not seem an impossible objective. Today it appears almost out of reach.

WAR AND PEACE

It is impossible to exaggerate the consequences of the al-Qaeda attack on the United States. The key decision, as I make clear in my sixth chapter on 'War and Peace', was made very quickly, the decision to treat terrorism not as an international crime against humanity, but as an act of war. Instead of siting this terrible act within the context of the new post-national rule of law, and demanding a common response by all law-abiding world citizens, the Bush administration reverted to the familiar Westphalian pattern of nation against nation. It found in Afghanistan the rogue government that had apparently fostered and protected the terrorist network.

It is not easy to fit a shadowy global network bent on destruction of innocent people into this traditional system. What nations bear responsibility? Failed states can claim that their writ does not run. Fragile states that are ethnically or religiously divided can argue that their unity could be put at risk by suppressing militant activity. Powerful states identify themselves with the war on terrorism, sidestepping their own past involvement in training or financing terrorist activities. The United States, which armed and trained the mujahedin of Afghanistan and Pakistan against the Soviet Union, and sold arms to Iraq in the dreadful Iraq–Iran war, has a particular responsibility to investigate its own contribution to the hydra-headed enemy, terrorism.

I wish terrorism had been defined as an international crime. I wish it had been coupled with other international crimes like genocide, ethnic cleansing, the systematic use of rape and torture and, something not yet treated as a crime, the ravaging of the planet's resources against the interests of the planet's inhabitants. I wish we in the West – not just the United States – had tackled our own complicity in laundering dirty money, in selling arms to misgoverned and divided countries and in controlling the trade in oil, gold and diamonds, assets that could transform the prospects of the poorest countries in Africa.

It is easy to despair. The natural world has been subordinated to the imperatives of materialism. The calamitous acceleration in the destruction of species, that marvellous gift of creation known as biodiversity, and the warming of the planet are waymarks on the road to an environment that cannot sustain human life. Comfortably established in my green fragment of England, I cannot put out of my head the images of children swollen and dulled by hunger, peasant farmers staring at parched fields, and the endless ranks of the young dead, some doomed by AIDS, some by starvation, some by the consequences of their own deluded fanaticism. Meanwhile, the forests are still being burned and slashed, the soil is still being washed into the rivers, and the children are still drinking polluted water.

There are of course some answers. A few countries and corporations are investing public and private money imaginatively. A few economists are criticizing the desperately unjust distribution of the world's wealth and resources; some even argue for a carbon tax, or a Tobin tax on international capital movements. Hundreds of thousands of people devote their energies and talents to helping the 'wretched of the earth' or to rebuilding shattered societies. Some of these good people try to follow the teaching of Jesus Christ in lives of service to their neighbours.

So while the challenge of evil is very great, evil in our nations and ourselves as well as in 'the other', the menacing stranger we know little about, there is also great potential force for good. The good among us often distrust power, and power in turn underestimates moral and spiritual force. But I have seen that force, in the hands of men and women without material or political power, move nations.

THE KINGDOM OF GOD

When the media want to describe my being a Catholic, they often use the word 'devout'. The word suggests someone who does not question his or her faith, who has abdicated from the harrowing dominion of doubt. What the media probably mean is that I go to church most Sundays, and occasionally mention God. I am, however, a person of my times, and therefore in this secular society, beset by doubt. Of all the apostles, the one I find most congenial is St Thomas. They called him 'doubting Thomas'. He must have been of a scientific disposition, since he would not accept the word of Jesus about the Resurrection without proof. Only when he saw the hands and the side of the crucified Christ, was he able to declare his conviction, 'My Lord and my God'. My own position is like that of the man whose son was wracked with convulsions, who met Jesus after the transfiguration. Jesus declared, 'Everything is possible to the one who has faith'. The man responded, 'I have faith. Help me where faith falls short.' My own prayer is similar. 'Lord, I believe; help Thou my unbelief.'

The Church aligned itself with the good, with the force of love, for a few brief and blessed years during the pontificate of John XXIII. That memory is still with us, a glimpse of light in a darkening prospect. It was a triumph of faith over the calculations of power and advantage made over centuries by the leaders of the Catholic Church. So the Holy Spirit still moves among us – and perhaps may move even through the defensive walls of the Vatican.

Chapter 1

The Church in the Modern World

Let me begin with a word of warning. Much of this first chapter is about the distancing of human beings in the contemporary developed world from their Creator. Modern secular societies are self-absorbed and self-contained, seeing the spiritual dimension of human beings as a private matter for each individual. Social relationships and the norms that govern them are no longer central to many of these individuals. Modern information technology enables them to create their own microworlds of virtual friends and colleagues.

I shall argue that scientific, technological and economic advances offer better explanations for the secularization of modern society than sin, though they may also open up new occasions for evil conduct. They present a challenge that those of us who are practising Christians have yet to meet. Indeed, we are in danger of castigating and condemning them, like so many Canutes ordering the tides to turn back.

THE PARADOX

There is, however, a paradox that I cannot explain. The

United States, like Europe and the rest of the developed world, has welcomed advances in science and technology, and enjoyed the fruits of material abundance they have brought. Yet the decline in religious belief and practice in the United States is much less dramatic than it is in Europe. A very large majority of Americans claim to believe in God, in the Incarnation and in an afterlife. Of Europe, the Pope himself has spoken of a reversion to paganism. Outside ecclesiastical circles, the description 'post-Christian' is often used to describe that continent.

Secularization in my own homeland has gone so far – despite, or perhaps because of, the existence of established churches, the Church of England and in Scotland, the Presbyterian Church – that fewer than one person in ten is a regular Church attender. The decline of religious practice in the United States is much less dramatic than it is in Europe. A very large majority of Americans believe in the fundamental Christian doctrines, and regularly go to Church.

The evidence is clear and dramatic. The Victorian era in Britain was dominated by the Church of England and the evangelical Nonconformist churches, Methodist, Baptist, Congregationalist and others. Most families married in church and baptized their children. Women were seen as 'instruments of piety' and attended church in a ratio twice that of men. The double standard of social and sexual morality obtained, a strict standard for women, a much more relaxed and forgiving standard for men. Until the 1870s, most boys and girls were educated in Church schools. Many still are. They were enrolled in youth organizations with a distinctly Christian flavour, the Church Army, the Boys' Brigade, the Boy Scouts and Girl Guides of that era. Political parties, though never formally associated, were linked in the public mind with particular denominations.

Before the Second World War, the Church of England used to be described as the Conservative Party at prayer. The Labour Party, unlike its often anticlerical sister socialist parties in continental Europe, was said 'to owe more to Methodism than to Marxism', a tribute to its Nonconformist elements.[1]

Great Britain could reasonably be described as a Christian country until well after the Second World War. Indeed, churchgoing actually rose in the post-war years between 1945 and 1959, years of austerity but also of hope. But some time around the beginning of the 1960s, that defining decade, everything changed. People's standard of living began to improve rapidly as shortages were overcome. Television became widely available. The invention of the Pill broke the biological link between sexual intercourse and procreation, ushering in a new age of freedom for women. Harold Wilson's reforming government of 1966–70 supported Private Members' Bills to legalize homosexual relations between adult men, as well as abortion in the early stages of pregnancy. Censorship of plays and films was relaxed. And in Rome, a second Vatican Council proposed changes in the attitudes and practices of the Roman Catholic Church that were breathtaking in their scope and in their consequences.

Whether *post hoc* or *propter hoc*, church attendance in Great Britain began to fall dramatically. Some observers attributed the fall in church attendance among Roman Catholics to the changes in the Mass and the relaxation of rules sanctioned by the Second Vatican Council. That decline was, however, more marked among Anglicans than among Roman Catholics, and it is open to question how substantial an impact the Second Vatican Council had on them.

Throughout the last twenty years of the nineteenth century and the first fifty-five of the twentieth, the number of Easter communicants, the benchmark of membership in the Church of England, had declined almost impercept- ibly, by 0.26 per cent, around a quarter of one per cent, each year. Between 1956 and 1984, the figure multiplied five times to 1.3 per cent a year. By the latter year, Easter communicants had dropped to two-fifths of the 1900 figure.[2]

The figures for the Roman Catholic population, and for regular Mass attenders among them, are not wholly reliable. There is no formal national census, and the figures that do exist are compiled from parish reports. The Catholic population of Great Britain in 1999 was estimated to be 4,855,262, of whom about a quarter attended Mass regularly, a modest decline from 1988, the earliest date for which Mass attendances were estimated.[3] Much more serious has been the drop in vocations – 43 per cent for female religious, 82 per cent for male religious and 54 per cent for male seminarians between 1965 and 1995. But such figures are far from unprecedented in Europe; figures for female religious in France, the Netherlands and Germany, and for seminarians in France and the Netherlands, show even greater declines.[4]

The solidity of Christian belief is strongly related to the practice of religion. Catholics in Britain, according to the BBC/*Tablet* survey,[5] believe, by a very large majority of 80 per cent or more, in the Incarnation and the Crucifixion, and, by a rather smaller majority of 73 per cent, in the Resurrection. These beliefs are rooted in much greater observance than that of all other Christian denominations except the small House Church movement. Catholics are now 11 per cent of the population of Great Britain, but 26 per cent of those attending religious services (other than weddings, funerals, etc.) once a month or more. Those who argue that attendance at Sunday Mass is vital to the health of Christian belief have solid evidence on their side. That is why the decline in vocations is so serious.

A SPIRITUAL YEARNING

These statistics are not intended to show that my fellow-citizens lack a spiritual sense, or indeed a spiritual hunger. The survey conducted in June 2000 by the BBC and the distinguished Catholic weekly, *The Tablet*, indicated that two-thirds of the British people thought they had souls, and that there was an afterlife, though, in our self-deluding age, twice as many believed in heaven as in hell. A surprisingly high proportion claimed to pray, and to believe that their prayers were answered.[6] Secular societies, as that eminent theologian Nicholas Lash has pointed out, are not necessarily irreligious societies. They are societies in which religious institutions have lost power and influence, and in which religious beliefs are held to be implausible and irrational. Nevertheless, the right of individuals to hold such beliefs is respected.

The Catholic writer G. K. Chesterton once said that the trouble when people stop believing in God is not that they thereafter believe in nothing, it is that they thereafter believe in anything.[7] The spiritual void in secular societies is filled by a mélange of dreams, emotions, pagan myths and a vague mysticism engendered by popularized versions of Asian religions, especially Buddhism and Hinduism. That mélange may be a spiritual accompaniment to globalization, a picking and choosing among religious ideas and experiences easily accessible through the proliferation of channels of communication and sources of information. Its attraction depends in part on some common ground between religious teachings. I offer only one example here, drawn from the *Bhagavad Gita*, which many might suppose came from the New Testament: 'Only by love can men know me, and see me, and come unto me.'

The secularized communities I live in respond to values such as respect for human rights, democracy, social justice (providing it is not too expensive), the duty to alleviate pain, poverty and suffering. They are not ungenerous societies. They are, however, suspicious of organized religion, resistant to unelected authority, with the exception of authority based on technical expertise, and worried about the direction the human race is taking. In short, they see religion as a private matter, while mourning the loss of its influence on family and society.

The disconnection between a vague aspiration to spirituality, on the one hand, and knowledge of Christianity and adherence to its institutions, on the other, appears to be characteristic of many modern Western societies. In some countries, even the Christian narrative, the bedrock common knowledge of the life and teaching of Jesus Christ and of fundamental Christian doctrine, is beginning to disappear.

In the autumn of 2000, during a lecture tour of Germany, I met a young West German in Leipzig, capital of the state of Brandenburg and home to the great Lutheran church, the Thomaskirche, in which Johann Sebastian Bach was for many years kapellmeister. The young man had married a girl from East Germany, brought up and educated in the Soviet era. One of the factors that eventually led to the breakdown of their marriage was the girl's total ignorance of the Christian story. She could not identify the statue of the Madonna on the façade of churches, nor did she know why she was there. The Crucifixion and the Resurrection meant nothing to her. She did not know who St Peter and St Paul were, nor what they had done. That is what I mean by the loss of the Christian narrative.

RELIGION IN AMERICA

Why did a similar decline in religious practice not occur in the United States? Let me hazard one or two observations, if only to encourage discussion. Christianity in the United States has been dominated by the pursuit of individual salvation, religion as a private matter, and that in turn has been underpinned by the formal separation of Church and state. James Madison said of that separation, 'Religion flourishes in greater purity without than with the aid of government.'[8] There is of course no state Church in the United States. In Britain, by contrast, the largest denomination, in terms of numbers, is Anglican (Episcopalian is the closest American analogy), the country's established church, united with the state through the monarch, who is 'Defender of the Faith' and head of both Church and state.

The existence of an established church in several European countries is an important distinction between them and the United States, with its constitutional separation of Church and state, but it is not necessarily the most significant one. The Roman Catholic Church in Europe has historically been deeply involved in politics and in civil society. In the United States, through schools, hospitals and religious charities, the Church has also had a significant social role. But it has been a minority Church, for a long time suspect because of its loyalty to an external authority, the Pope. Its bishops have concentrated on particular issues associated with the culture of life, opposition to abortion, euthanasia and capital punishment. There are Catholic politicians, but there are no specifically Catholic or Christian political parties as there are (or were) in Germany, Italy and elsewhere in Europe. The policies of these parties, influenced by Catholic social teaching, are much less conservative than those of the Christian Coalition in the United States.

The separation of Church and state may have fostered the emphasis on personal salvation characteristic of evangelical Christianity. As an alternative explanation for the remarkable levels of Christian practice in the United States, that emphasis on personal salvation may suit an individualistic modern age better than the message of the mainstream Christian denominations, still dominant in Western European Christianity. It is significant that evangelical Christianity has little sympathy for the social gospel. Yet for many Catholics, it expresses their aspiration to greater justice and compassion in this world. The social gospel has profoundly influenced the family and social policies of the European Community (now the European Union). It has had no equivalent effect on US social policy. This is a theme to which I shall return.

There is, however, a third possible explanation, some-what at odds with the others. Separation of Church and state there may have been, but in a sense the United States itself took on a sacred status. It is, after all, one of the few countries founded by men and women driven by religious convictions, and determined to make of their new land a model for all others to follow. The Puritan John Winthrop, crossing the Atlantic, spoke of the new settlements as like a city on a hill, 'the eyes of all people are upon us'. Cotton Mather spoke of 'a scripture-pattern that shall in due time be accomplished the whole world throughout'.[9]

This sense of mission illuminated and inspired the Founding Fathers, a suggestive name for a group of remarkable politicians who spent much time discussing the place of religion in their new nation. It survives to the present day, in the powerful symbolism of flag and anthem, and in the recital of the Pledge of Allegiance by schoolchildren in most public schools. It is manifest, too, in the presence of the flag in many public places, including churches and town halls, in the offices of senators and representatives, and in countless Stars and Stripes flying outside American homes. In Europe, the harsh lessons of history have led to a deep distrust of those who proclaim a national mission. Rarely does one see the national flag flying even in the office of a public servant. When it happens in a private place in Britain, the homeowner is usually either an Ulsterman or a passionate Euro-sceptic.

I turn now to the impact of the contemporary world on religious belief in general, and on Christianity in particular. Those of us in public life who are Christians must strive to understand the changes we have to contend with, and how the Gospel of Christ pertains to them. Whichever side of the Atlantic we may be on, and whatever the social context, we must be conscious of their impact and think through our response to them.

THE STANDARD OF LIVING

Scientific and technological advances have brought to the populations of the Western world in the last half century an almost unimaginable leap in their material standard of living. When I was a little girl in England, just before the Second World War, life for most people was not greatly different from that of the late Victorian age. The houses of the majority, the so-called 'working class', had no running hot water, no central heating, no television, no refrigerator, no freezer, no washing machine and an outside toilet in the backyard. Most men worked at hard manual jobs, digging, ploughing, building, mining. As late as 1938, some 791,000 men in Great Britain still worked in the coal mines. Women worked in the textile mills or were employed in large numbers as cooks, maids and washerwomen. They washed clothes by boiling them in coppers, wringing them through mangles and pegging them out to dry. They scrubbed and polished by hand, and humped wood and coal for the fires and kitchen ranges. By mid-life, women and men alike were worn out, suffering the aches and pains of a hard life; yet the pensions they could expect were derisory, and the health care rudimentary.

Within two generations after the war, life at work and in the home was transformed. Labour-saving machines cut out much of the daily drudgery in the home and outside it. There was an abundance of choice. Furthermore, this material transformation was accompanied by massive social change, sweeping away traditional barriers to aspirations to fortune, career and status. The removal of these barriers was most marked in the case of women, but also extended to birthplace and social class. (It has yet to be fully realized for race and religion.) The welfare state, constructed during the war and greatly extended in the following decade, removed the fear of destitution from the elderly, the disabled and the sick, and established a minimum social safety net for everyone.

ABUNDANCE

Abundance of choice is the distinguishing characteristic of economically advanced societies. The ability of manufacturers and service providers to tailor their products to individual tastes makes consumption a much more exciting activity than it was in the early days of mass production, when everyone bought his or her own identical Model T Ford car. Materialism has been raised to a sophisticated level. Cardinal Hume of Westminster once described consumerism as the new religion. 'For many people, shopping,' he said, 'has become a powerful source of meaning and fulfilment'.[10] Admittedly, shopping can become an addiction, a sad way to pursue happiness. But it can also be satisfying, as people spend time, money, thought and energy on improving their homes, their health, their appearance and their children's development. They no longer need to look outwards from cramped and wretched lives to find their inspiration and consolation in God and the afterlife. At the very least, it takes a while to appreciate the hollowness in material riches, an anomie that cannot be filled by more of the same.

Even so, it is selfish to denigrate the material advances of the last two centuries. Tellingly, such denigration often comes from those who are well-off themselves. It is good that people are healthier, cleaner, warmer, better fed and enjoy such a spectrum of opportunity. It is good that they take such pride in their homes and in their children. And it is challenging for Christians that they can no longer rely on poverty and misery in this world as reasons for yearning for the next. We have to find other ways to make the Gospel of Christ relevant to our lives.

THE LOSS OF GAIA

The scientist James Lovelock wrote a book called *Gaia: A New Look at Life on Earth*, after the Greek name of the goddess who represented the planet earth in all its beauty.[11] The book's cover was the famous photograph of the earth seen from outer space, a small blue and green planet wreathed by white clouds, touching in its fragility in the infinite cosmos. Gaia has become the source of a cult in the modern world, seized upon by Green activists and New Age modern pagans. But construed as a straightforward metaphor, the Gaia legend evokes recognition of the interconnectedness of everything within the organism that is planet earth, and the need to recognize and treasure that delicate balance. The new catechism of the Catholic Church puts it well: 'a religious respect for the integrity of creation'. Gradually, economists and physicists are coming to acknowledge its importance.

Respect for God's creation, indeed its celebration, has long been a reason for reverence. The Gaia myth today symbolizes the awe and wonder of the natural world. To understand that, look at a little child exploring the countryside. One of my abiding images is my eighteen-month-old grandson running into the sunlight with his arms held out wide, embracing the sky and the green garden. Another treasured image is a hidden side canyon of the great Colorado River, unapproachable except from the river itself, a miniature Eden almost untouched by man, of huge rocks, luxuriant plants and crystal rock pools.

For centuries, the world of nature has provided human beings with spiritual as well as material nourishment. Listen to these voices: William Wordsworth in 1807 in his ode, 'Intimations of Immortality' from Recollections of Early Childhood:

> There was a time when meadow, grove and stream,
> The earth, and every common sight,
> To me did seem
> Apparell'd in celestial light ...
>
> Poems in Two Volumes (1807)

And the priest-poet, Gerald Manley Hopkins, in 1877:

> *God's Grandeur*
> The world is charged with the grandeur of God.
>   It will flame out, like shining from shook foil;

It gathers to a greatness, like the ooze of oil
Crushed. Why do men then now not reck his rod?
Generations have trod, have trod, have trod;
   And all is seared with trade; bleared, smeared with
   toil;
   And wears man's smudge and shares man's smell:
   the soil
Is bare now, nor can foot feel, being shod.

And for all this, nature is never spent;
   There lives the dearest freshness deep down things;
And though the last lights off the black West went,
   Oh, morning, at the brown brink eastward, springs –
Because the Holy Ghost over the bent
   World broods with warm breast and with ah! bright
   wings.

These poets felt themselves to be at one with the natural world. They encountered, in natural phenomena like thunderstorms, floods and blizzards, and even in the procession of the seasons, a sense of the power of the Almighty. That sense of awe is still to be found among people who live close to the earth, the indigenous people, whether in Africa, Amazonia or remote rural areas of our own countries. But most of us in the advanced industrialized countries are distanced from the natural world. The storm beats on our double-glazed windows as we pull the curtains, so that we neither see nor hear it. Electricity has long since banished darkness, and with that the mystery of night images, the moon laced in the branches of trees, the distant hoot of owls. Just as the sodium lights of the highway blot out the stars, so God seems hazy and far away.

The rural landscapes which inspired Wordsworth and Hopkins and many other poets were man-made and had been for a very long time. But the industrialization of agriculture has ended the ancient dialogue of man and nature, replacing it with a radical and impatient exploitation of the earth. When I was a girl, I was evacuated to Cambridge for several months from my bombed school. The old house where I stayed was in a quiet road that led into a big wheat field, scattered with scarlet poppies and blue cornflowers. I used to lie among the wheat ears for hours, looking up at the huge clouds processing across the big East Anglian sky, listening to the skylarks singing their hearts out as they climbed towards the light. They inspired the composer Ralph Vaughan Williams' *The Lark Ascending* (*Romance for violin and orchestra*). The quiet road is still there, but the wild flowers are few and the skylarks have gone.

Sometimes human beings seem a lone species rather than part of the rest of creation. Our mastery over the planet, and now into space, feeds the human sense of uniqueness. Shakespeare's 'poor, bare forked animal' can walk on the moon, investigate Mars, unravel the secrets of the genetic code and create virtual worlds to his own design. This is the age of Prometheus, when men aspire to become gods.

But alongside our ability to create is our ability to destroy. When Robert Oppenheimer saw at Alamogordo, New Mexico, in July 1945, the first atom bomb explosion flower into a sinister mushroom cloud, he whispered the words inspired by the Hindu scriptures, the *Bhagavad Gita*, 'I am become death, the destroyer of worlds.'[12] Science has provided us with massively greater powers, but our moral sense of how to use those powers has not similarly developed. Pride, or, to use a better word, what the Greeks called *hubris*, remains the first of the cardinal sins, and lies in wait for the new Prometheans.

For the most elemental choice, that between good and evil, still confronts human beings in this modern age. The nuclear bomb exemplified humanity's ability to destroy the planet; the Holocaust, the genocides in Rwanda, Cambodia and the Balkans, its readiness to do so. It is difficult to deny the presence of evil in our modern world. But it is also difficult to impose limits on what our knowledge aspires to, the Promethean ambition for men to become God.

Let me conclude by reiterating my main argument, that scientific and technological advances, and the material abundance associated with them, have distanced human beings from God and from His creation, the natural world. The consequences are far from being all bad, but they do present Christians and other believers with new, and so far, unmet challenges. The choice between doing good or evil with our knowledge remains, in the modern world as in the past. The Gospel of Christ, and the explication of His life and His teaching, provide us with the basis for that moral choice.

NOTES

1. Morgan Phillips, General Secretary of the Labour Party, quoted in *Time and Chance*, the autobiography of James Callaghan (London: Collins, 1987).
2. Callum G. Brown, *The Death of Christian Britain* (London: Routledge, 2001).
3. The Catholic Media Office, London; figures compiled from annual Catholic directories, 2000.
4. Rodney Stark and Roger Finke, 'Catholic Religious Vocation: Decline and Revival', *Review of Religious Research, 2000*, Vol. 42, No. 2, pp. 125–45.
5. *The Soul of Britain*, a survey conducted in June 2000 by Opinion Research Business for the BBC Radio 4 *Sunday* programme and *The Tablet*, special report 14 April 2001.
6. Ibid.
7. First recorded as 'The first effect of not believing in God is to

believe in anything', in Emile Cammaerts, *Chesterton: The Laughing Prophet* (London: Methuen & Co., 1937).

8. G. Hunt (ed.), *The Writings of James Madison*, 1910, Vol. 1 (New York: G. Putnam).

9. Quoted in Arthur Schlesinger Jr, address at the inauguration of Vartan Gregorian as President of Brown University, printed in *The New York Times Book Review*, 23 July 1989.

10. Cardinal Basil Hume, the fifteenth annual Arnold Goodman Charity Lecture, June 1998.

11. James Lovelock, *Gaia: A New Look at Life on Earth* (Oxford: OUP, 1979).

12. Oppenheimer's recollection was not wholly accurate. The actual phrase from the *Bhagavad Gita* is '*I (Krishna) am all-powerful Time, which destroys all things, and I have come here to slay these men.*'

Chapter 2

The Death of Deference

What has happened to deference, the traditional respect of people for those above them in the social, generational or religious hierarchy, whether the young for the old, the less educated for the more educated or the poorer for the richer? My thesis is that deference of this kind has died in most Western societies, and consequently cannot be relied upon by the mainstream churches or by secular society as the basis for an institutional hierarchy.

For centuries before the Enlightenment, the authority of the Church, or of secular powers recognized by the Church's hierarchy, sufficed for Christian societies to accept the validity of a doctrine or statement promulgated by them. The poet W. H. Auden encapsulated the spirit of those centuries in his sonnet, 'The Age of Faith':

> *The History of Truth*:
> In that ago, when being was believing
> Truth was the most of many credibles
> More first, more always, than a bat-winged
> lion
> A fish-tailed dog or eagle-headed fish
> The least like mortals, doubted by their deaths

Truth was their model as they strove to build
A world of lasting objects to believe in,
Without believing earthenware and legend,
Archway and song, were truthful or untruthful:
The Truth was there already to be true.

This while when, practical like paper-dishes
Truth is convertible to kilowatts,
Our last to do by is an anti-model,
Some untruth anyone can give the lie to,
A nothing no one need believe is there.

W. H. Auden, Collected Poems
Faber & Faber (1976)

In our post-Enlightenment era, more than simply external authority is required. In the words of Nicholas Lash in *Voices of Authority*: 'an appeal to external criteria is likely to be unsuccessful in the measure that the proposition on behalf of which such an appeal is made lacks internal authority; lacks, that is, the self-authenticating authority of perceived truth.'[1]

If external authority no longer suffices without the corroboration of experience, or because the proposition advanced by external authority convinces us in its own terms that it is sensible or wise, the weakening of traditional respect further undermines it. Neither external authority nor traditional deference can be relied upon as the foundation of institutional hierarchy. To show how great the change has been, let me recall the importance of deference in my own country a century or so ago.

Mid-nineteenth-century England was an orderly society; people knew their place. Society resembled one of those dovecotes you can still see hidden behind or alongside the manor house in old English and French villages. Dovecotes are wooden birdhouses in which doves live, consisting of horizontal rows of nesting boxes, neatly placed one above the other, thereby creating vertical rows as well. Each nesting box is inhabited by a dove who knows its exact place in the pecking order. Doves, unlike cuckoos, are not revolutionary birds. Traditionally, they symbolize peace.

Doves are not human beings. But the sense that order and peace are related underpinned the social hierarchy of Victorian England. Note the third verse of a popular hymn of the time, 'All Things Bright and Beautiful':

> The rich man in his castle,
> The poor man at the gate,
> He made them, high and lowly,
> And ordered their estate.

> *C. F. Alexander, (1848)*

The Victorian social hierarchy was solidly based on class, wealth and education, though in England (unlike Scotland), the last of these, education, counted for much less than class and wealth. My maternal grandmother, born in Aberystwyth in 1868, the high noon of Victorian England, had managed to pull herself out of genteel poverty by marrying the eldest son of a prosperous Staffordshire family. But she would have been shocked at the idea of her daughter, my mother, marrying 'into trade', what today we would call business or commerce. Better by far to marry a landowner or army officer, or even a vicar, though his stipend would not match the trader's income. The United States was, of course, much less class-bound, but not entirely so, at least on the east coast, as the novels of Henry James and Edith Wharton testify.

As well as class, Victorian England was comfortable in its unshakeable conviction that it deserved and possessed the

41

top nest in the dovecote, above all other nations and all other races. Its middle-class young men bore the burden of teaching others how to live, governing them and converting the lesser breeds in its vast empire to the English under-standing of what constituted Christian civilization. Few doubted their national mission, and many admired their leaders for their achievements and experience. They might have echoed Isaac Newton's tribute to his forefathers: 'If I see far, it is because I stand on other men's shoulders.'[2]

THE ROLE OF EDUCATION

In England and Wales, the Church of England had increased its influence in a slowly democratizing society by its important role in the education of the people. State funding subsidized free Church-controlled elementary schools as early as 1833, significantly just after the passage of the first Reform Act extending the franchise. It was 1870 before free public elementary (grade school) education was introduced. The Church of England even after that retained its important position in public education, and to this day controls or manages a quarter of the elementary schools of England and Wales.[3] The Lord's Prayer is said in every such school, Church or state, on most school days.

The Roman Catholic Church's influence in continental Europe was similarly bolstered by its key role in education. For the promising but poor boy, for many centuries the road to becoming a cleric, and with it acquiring status and influence, ran by way of the Church. For young women with limited prospects, becoming a religious sister opened the doors of education and opportunity. In its seminaries and abbeys, the young monk or seminarian would learn Latin, the lingua franca or common language of Western Christianity, Greek, geometry and arithmetic, classical and contemporary literature, philosophy, grammar, music, astronomy and theology.[4] If he were an able scholar, he might move on to one of the great centres of learning that flourished in the Middle Ages and beyond, supported and encouraged by the Church. Even in modern times, many schools and colleges in North America and Western Europe have been religious foundations, often staffed by men and women religious who commanded respect not only for their learning, but also for their vocations.

As servants of the Church, local bishops and priests shared in this respect. Their dioceses and parishes looked to them for leadership, example and advice. To be a priest was to have an honourable vocation, one that conferred local standing on his family. In societies that were illiterate or semi-literate, as most were until late in the nineteenth century, priests' education made them indispensable channels of communication to those higher up the pecking order. As for bishops, many held sway over substantial land and property. Often appointed after consultation with secular leaders, and sometimes with local communities, bishops were close to their people, and represented their interests to the Church's hierarchy, and to the secular power.

Today, in our modern educated Western democracies, deference to hierarchy, secular or religious, has almost disappeared. Among the reasons, as well as those advanced above, is the loss of the Churches' dominant position in education, which in any case never obtained in the United States. (In the colonial period, there had been a brief theocracy in the Massachusetts Bay colony, in which schooling was entirely run by the Puritans, but it disappeared long before Independence.)

By the last quarter of the nineteenth century, primary education had become compulsory in most American states and in most Western European countries. Governments recognized that an industrial economy required basic literacy to understand the instructions of management and to be able to make use of new inventions. Most of the new schools were financed by national, state or local governments. They were secular schools. In the United States and France, these state-financed schools were separate from the Churches. In the United Kingdom, primary education was provided by both Church and state schools, largely financed from public funds, and regulated by the same or similar provisions as to curriculum, examinations and term times.

Increasingly sophisticated methods of production and the growth of service industries demanded more advanced education. The post-Second World War period in the industrialized countries was the occasion for a massive expansion in secondary education. The period of compulsory education was stretched, in most such countries, from eight or nine years to eleven or more. Many of those with secondary education in turn aspired to a still higher level, a university degree, opening the gateways to a professional career or a business qualification. In the 1950s and 1960s, the higher education sector in the industrialized countries doubled and trebled in size. Furthermore, earlier generations denied this opportunity demanded provision for mature students. Part-time degree courses and the Open University were two of the many responses to this new and vibrant market.

As generational and social barriers to higher education fell, the exclusiveness that higher education had once conferred began to weaken, and with it another of the privileges of the priesthood. Traditionalists found succour in the reputation of their universities or seminaries, especially those that were the oldest or most renowned. But higher education had ceased to be the secret garden of a small minority. The educational pyramid had become broader and less steep.

TECHNOLOGICAL AUTHORITY

Because rapid technological progress makes much of our knowledge swiftly obsolete, age and experience, with their heritage of learning, no longer attract respect. Who needs to know now how to harness a carriage horse, or how to take a letter down in shorthand? The cult of youth is not just a consequence of television and the advertising industry. It has a basis in the real world. After all, it is young people who pioneered the personal computer and the Internet, and built the dot.com empire, becoming rich and powerful, at least for a time, in the process. The market has consequently paid much attention to them, and to their children, for as parents they offer a vulnerable and responsive prospect. By contrast, the market pays little attention to age, except for those peddling cruises, pensions or retirement homes.

We, the members of these societies, do of course recognize and respect technical and professional expertise, like that of the doctor or the scientist, though the expert nowadays is likely to be questioned and asked to explain herself. People accept the need for interlocutors with increasingly sophisticated technical worlds, like that of computer science, and respect those who have mastered it. Such respect is based on empirical evidence. So, in a different way, is respect for good works, like those of a Mother Teresa or a Nelson Mandela. What is dying is deference towards hierarchy based on social or family relationships, which have underpinned political stability and ecclesiastical authority alike. The weakening of these relationships in an increasingly atomized society may have as much to do with the death of deference as all the other factors I have adduced.

PUBLIC LIFE

Respect for leading figures in public life, whether secular or religious, has been affected by the commercialization of the media, desperately pursuing ratings and circulation figures rather than reputation. The media today are both king-makers and kingbreakers, engaged in first acclaiming new celebrities, and then revealing the feet of clay they and past idols alike possess. Once-respected professionals, above all people engaged in public life, are natural targets. So are figures of formal authority but little power; the British Royal Family is a good example.

Politicians have so far suffered most from the attentions of the media. Their private lives and their families are subjected to minute examination, down to the behaviour of their children. Youthful indiscretions are dredged up from the sediment of the past. And if they yield, under stress, to bad behaviour, their weaknesses will feed the headline writers for days on end. The British newspapers relished the defensive jab landed by the Deputy Prime Minister, John Prescott, on a young man who assaulted him during a walkabout in the rather boring General Election in 2001. It kept them happy for days.

It is hard to say exactly when the private lives of political leaders became open books for the media. Certainly prominent politicians were accused of scandalous behaviour in the eighteenth and nineteenth centuries – President Cleveland and Prime Minister Palmerston come to mind. There were two important differences from now, however. Their own families, wives and children, were off-limits unless themselves involved in the scandal, and the journals were read by few outside the inner circle of politicians. The relentless exploitation of private lives for the titillation of the wider public is a new phenomenon, legitimated by the demand for openness in public matters, and by the success of the *Washington Post* in revealing President Nixon's role in Watergate. It has been further stimulated by the repeated indiscretions of former President Clinton. Today, every aspiring young journalist has a crusader's banner in his pocket.

The consequences of all this for political life are serious. Why should voters entrust major decisions to a legislature of elected representatives for whom they have no respect? The decline in voter turnout and the growing resort to direct action outside the formal democratic framework suggests that many no longer do. It would be alarmist to say that representative democracy is at risk, but it is undoubtedly far from healthy. So it is important for good young men and women to enter public life. I try to encourage them to do so. After all, my own experience of politics is that most of its practitioners are good and conscientious men and women.

I used to run a class at the John F. Kennedy School of Government, called 'To Be a Politician', a name deliberately copied from the title of a book on that subject which extolled the privilege of representing others and serving them. Towards the end of the session, I asked my students how the class had affected their ambition to enter public life. Many, to my consternation, had reluctantly concluded they could not do so. The main reason, overwhelmingly, was that they did not feel they could, or should, subject their children, spouses or parents to the attentions of the media.

For the Christian attracted to public life, the dilemma is acute. On the one hand, there is the call to serve society, and especially those of its members least able to look after themselves. On the other, there is the obligation to protect and cherish the family. But that is not the only dilemma. He or she is further aware that the whole profession has been demeaned, and is now among the least respected of occupations, paradoxically alongside journalism.

Considerations of family were not, of course, the only reason for my students' reluctance. The cost of elections at state and federal level in the United States is now ludicrously high. At the election in 2000, the average expenditure by the winner was $850,000 for a Congressional seat, and $5 million for the Senate, a figure that excludes from that average the extremely expensive races in New York and New Jersey.[5] Incumbents have to spend much of their time raising money for their next election, which rather removes the point of being elected in the first place.

In Britain, the cost of elections is held down by regulations strictly limiting the amount any candidate in a constituency can spend, and by the barring of candidates and campaigns from purchasing air time for radio or television presentations. Limited free time is allocated broadly on the basis of the share of the vote at the most recent General Election. But the raising of money by the parties for campaigning, other than through radio and television, is not prohibited, and wealthy donors are being wooed in Britain as in the United States. Money has become the key determinant of electability, not ability or character. That too feeds public cynicism. It is hardly surprising that some of the best among us no longer want to enter public life.

THE PRIESTHOOD

There are some obvious analogies between public life and the priesthood. Bishops and priests are no longer immune from the ferreting of the media. In a society without deference, it is not role or status but personal standards and good works that win trust and confidence. That is why revelations of priestly misbehaviour are so damaging. The Irish Catholic Church, according to close friends of mine in the priesthood there, is still struggling to recover from the shock, now nearly ten years ago, of learning that the popular Bishop Eamon Casey had fathered a child and used diocesan funds to defray some of the consequent expenses. The Western secular world, tolerant about itself, sentimentalizes priests and nuns, and is then scandalized when they fall short of an impossible ideal.

The Roman Catholic priesthood is in a critical condition, not only because of a shortage of vocations, but because of the hydra-headed scandal of sexual abuse of children by priests. By one estimate, as many as 2,000 priests in the United States currently stand accused of the abuse of children at some stage in their ministry.[6] Every case that is made known, however old, contributes to a sense of betrayal among the laity, who have been taught from infancy to respect priests. How is that possible when priests themselves are involved in one of the most wretched of crimes?

What has made the scandal much worse has been the evidence of bishops either ignoring information provided to them about misbehaving priests, or even deliberately trying to conceal the facts. Accusations have not been treated with the seriousness they deserve, nor victims with the compassion they need. One such victim, Frank Martinelli of Stamford, Connecticut, told the journalist who interviewed him for *Time* Magazine that he did not want cash, but a public apology.[7] Leaders of the Church should surely understand that better than most. Offering cash for silence is not the behaviour expected of the shepherds of souls.

Yet one should spare a thought for the majority of priests who remain loyal to their vocation at a time when that is much harder than it used to be. On the one hand, celibacy and obedience are no longer appreciated by a society that does not greatly value them, that may even regard them as an aberration. On the other hand, the young priest is beset by images of material abundance and personal success, of sensuality and eroticism, that may weaken his commitment to his vocation. He can no longer count on the respect for that vocation once accorded by his community. Even good Catholic families are no longer sure they want to rejoice when their son or daughter wishes to be a priest or a nun.

There are those who argue strongly that Vatican II, in equating the status of the religious with that of the laity, removed the main incentive for a religious vocation. Many people are indeed drawn by the demands of obedience and self-sacrifice, but need around them the strength and support of a close-knit community.[8] For diocesan priests, loneliness must be one of the main reasons for men abandoning their vocation. Furthermore, in today's Church the priest may well be on his own, in charge of one or more parishes, not one of a team or even one of a small group of priests sharing one another's worries and difficulties.

Father Alan Phillip, a Passionist priest from California of thirty years' standing, expressed that with great sensitivity in a recent article in *The Tablet*:

> If a person is called only to the priesthood, but not to celibacy, they should be told the truth: expect a lifelong struggle ... Every priest realizes, as Blaise Pascal said, that in the human person there is an abyss that only God can fill ... What a lot of us didn't know, but have come to experience more each passing year, is that there is also a 'near abyss' that only another human being can fill.[9]

Like many other lay people, I marvel at the perseverance of so many of our priests.

Unquestionably, there are social factors as well. The role of the priest is more limited than it once was, at least in economically developed societies. His advice on matters of politics, education, career and even personal relationships is no longer regarded as authoritative. There is now a large profession of secular counsellors and advisors who can claim expert knowledge of these areas. Furthermore, personal conscience is respected above institutional rules or doctrines.

Short of a massive recession or an ecological disaster, it is hard to see the present decline in vocations in the developed world changing for the better. It is not only the quantity of priests that is a matter of concern, though many parishes are now served by deacons and lay ministers. It is the average age of serving priests, which indicates a worsening position in the future.

Parishes in Western Europe are already recruiting priests from as far away as the Philippines and Sri Lanka. Vocations are increasing in Africa, Asia and Latin America, but not sufficiently to meet the needs of the millions of Catholics in these continents. The faithful of Africa and Latin America are so denuded of priests they are lucky to celebrate the Eucharist once a month or even less frequently. Driven by the shortage of priests, some bishops have not insisted on absolute loyalty to the rule of celibacy. Priests may be known in their own locality to have mistresses, or to be practising homosexuals. Rather than confront the crisis – which could mean accepting married priests, women priests and actively homosexual priests in stable relationships – the Vatican simply looks the other way. In the words of a largely sympathetic survey of the state of the Roman Catholic Church, *The Economist* commented: 'by mishandling sex, or trying to ignore it, the Church has hurt its authority in general.'[10]

Concealment, however, in particular about the incidence of paedophilia among priests, has done immense damage to the reputation of the Catholic hierarchy. The Vatican seems to hide from itself that there are instances of child abuse by priests, just as it hides from itself the extensive resort to contraception among Catholic married couples. Yet greater openness might well show that the incidence of paedophilia among the clergy has been exaggerated. Certain methods of investigation put a premium on the accuser, and, after the passage of many years, it can be almost impossible to establish the truth, one way or the other, about allegations of sexual abuse. There are thousands of priests who lead dedicated, blameless lives of service who are deeply hurt by such allegations. They deserve to be heard rather than disregarded.

What business of ours are these painful matters, the hierarchy might ask. It is our business because we are, as lay people, much affected. We are affected by the lack of priests. We are affected, and rightly so, by the new demands made on the laity for carrying an increasing share of what used to be the functions of priests, raising funds, visiting the sick and the elderly, bringing Holy Communion to them, running charities. We are affected by the scapegoating of certain priests for child abuse, because our own children or those of our friends may be pupils at the school or altar boys and girls in the parish. We are affected as politicians, because our constituents come and talk to us about whether unpleasant facts have been hushed up, or, on the contrary, innocent priests and teachers have seen their reputations destroyed.

In my previous constituency and elsewhere, I have been busily engaged in finding out whether police methods of inquiry are fair alike to the alleged victim and to the accused, some of them teachers in Catholic schools, some of them social workers and child carers. How can I pretend to be an ignorant lay person when in my own life I am not? And when I might have something useful to contribute to the problems confronting my Church?

Like other lay people, I yearn for a more open dialogue between 'the people of God', the bishops and the Vatican. There is tremendous vigour and commitment in many parishes. It is uplifting to see how the relationship between priests and people in such parishes can illuminate and draw together the life of a congregation. Bishops who are close to their priests and people bring to the Bishops' Conferences a sympathy and understanding of their burdens and their hopes that can be deeply impressive. But, during the long and in many ways remarkable Papacy of John Paul II, the promise of greater collegiality implicit in Vatican II has withered. The Vatican's administration of the Church has become increasingly centralized, blighting the prospect of spiritual renewal. The Curia, to whom much power has been delegated by Pope John Paul II, intent on his pastoral mission to the world, is secretive, conservative and rigid. In the words of the Catholic writer Maurice West, quoted in the *Economist* survey: 'The Church will lose many souls because the men in authority want to save their faces, and sometimes to save the faces of dead men.'[11]

The educated laity is open-minded about change. The survey conducted by the sociologists Father Andrew Greeley of the University of Chicago and Michael Hout of the University of California at Berkeley, in 1997, in six countries, indicated broad support among Catholics for certain reforms, foremost among them the election of bishops and the appointment of lay advisors.[12] In the economically developed countries, there was also majority support for married priests. On every proposal surveyed, younger and better educated Catholics were more in favour of change than their less-educated elders.

The 'people of God' today may still be sheep, but they are educated and inquiring sheep. They have grown up. They have become used to being treated, in the democracies in which many of them live, as adults having both rights and obligations. The asymmetry between the human rights Catholics enjoy as citizens in the secular world, guaranteed by law, and the absence of rights as members of the Church, is unsustainable. In the cases of those brought before the Congregation for the Doctrine of the Faith for unorthodox or heretical writings or statements, even the appropriate right to be informed of the charges against him or her, the presumption of innocence and a fair trial, are excluded. Some of the Church's most challenging and stimulating thinkers have been put in this position.

No one expects the Church to be a democratic institution in the secular political sense. Indeed, most Roman Catholics accept the religious authority of the Pope, the bishops and the *sensus fidelium*. But a Church whose pre-eminent leader so eloquently preaches human rights and the exercise of charity in the secular world should surely practise that preaching itself.

External authority on its own will not suffice in a modern world with little respect for age, experience or social status. That is not necessarily a bad thing. But it means we cannot rely any more on hierarchy to retain the respect of lay people, whether they are members of the Church or electors in a democratic state. Men and women in leadership positions now have to earn their trust and practise accountability to them. They can no longer assume it.

NOTES

1. Nicholas Lash, *Voices of Authority* (London: Sheed and Ward, 1976).
2. 'If I have seen further it is by standing on shoulders of giants.' Letter to Robert Hooke, 5 February 1676, in H. W. Turnbull (ed.), *Correspondence of Isaac Newton*, Vol. 1 (1959).
3. The Church of England had 4,505 primary (K–6) schools in January 2002; the total number of primary schools was 17,985. The Roman Catholic Church had 1,752 primary schools in England in January 2002, about a tenth of all such schools. Source: *Statistics of Education – Schools in England (2002)*, Office of National Statistics, UK.
4. G. Benson Clough, *A Short History of Education*, 2nd edn (London: 1904), chapter 1, part 2.
5. These figures are from The Campaign Finance Institute, Washington DC.
6. 'The Faith of the Fathers', *The Economist*, 21 May 2002.
7. 'Can the Church Be Saved?', by Johanna McGeary, *Time* Magazine, 24 March 2002.
8. Rodney Stark and Roger Finke, 'Catholic Religious Vocation: Decline and Revival', *Reviews of Religious Research*, 2000, Vol. 42, No. 2, pp. 125–45.
9. 'The Truth About Priests', Alan Phillip, *The Tablet*, 14 July 2001.
10. 'Between This World and the Next', *The Economist* (US Edition), 29 January 2001.
11. Ibid.
12. 'The People Cry Reform', Andrew Greeley and Michael Hout, *The Tablet*, 22 March 1997.

Chapter 3

Enter Eve

The consequences for politics, society and the Christian churches of the women's revolution of the 1960s is in my view best described in the words of a Catholic pamphlet, *The Culture of Life*, as 'the collective transformation of the consciousness of women'.[1] But that is a pretty ponderous phrase I shall attempt to explain. I will begin with some personal recollections of past attitudes.

When I left my highly academic, single-sex girls' school at the age of seventeen, with all the heady freedom of a 'gap year' ahead of me, I decided to learn from experience how other people lived, people well outside the specialized world of politics, literature and intellectual dialogue inhabited by my parents. I started by working on a farm, as an assistant cowman to a herd of Ayrshire cattle, patient red and white beasts with liquid eyes. I had to get up at 4.30 in the morning, and be in the milking parlour by 5.00, to attach the milking machine to each cow in turn, and then to finish off the milking by hand. It was a routine operation, so there was a chance to talk to my superior, the cowman himself, as I went on with the work.

My colleague, the cowman, was a committed Methodist. He inquired, pleasantly enough, what my religion was. 'I'm a Catholic,' I said, which was not strictly true, because, although my father was a Catholic, he did not believe in infant baptism, and I had not yet reached the age of majority at which I would be free to choose. There was a heavy silence, and then the clatter of the milk stool on the dairy floor. 'I can't work with a Catholic,' the cowman declared, and stormed out of the milking parlour to tell the farm manager of his principled stand.

Several years later, after I had graduated from university, I was invited to take part in a conference of young Christians from all over Europe who were engaged in politics. We were invited one evening to an abbey near Bruges in Belgium for dinner. During the meal, a lively discussion broke out about the role of Christian democracy in the construction of the new European Community, a discussion in which I, the only woman in the group, took vigorous part. The abbot surveyed me with growing disapproval. Finally, down the long polished refectory table, he sent skidding a full bottle of red wine. 'Those who try to speak like men,' he thundered, 'must learn to drink like men'.

The final story in this miniature trilogy was about an occurrence at the prestigious Brompton Oratory in London. By now a young journalist at *The Financial Times*, Britain's serious-minded equivalent to the *Wall Street Journal*, I was appointed by the local authority for London, the London County Council, as a lay governor. In Britain at that time, almost all the costs of parochial schools were met from public funds (85 per cent of capital expenditure and 100 per cent of recurrent expenditure), and a minority of governors were appointed by the local councils to each school's governing body. The Labour-dominated council had shown some sensitivity in appointing only Catholics to represent them on the governing body.

Proud of my new and responsible position, I turned up at the side door of the formidable Oratory to be confronted by an old, grumpy and gnarled doorkeeper. I told him I was the new governor. 'I know who you are,' he said. 'Follow me.' He put me in a small whitewashed cell, and told me he would come back when the governors were ready for me. After some twenty minutes he came back, and led me into the room where the governors met. Ten minutes later, after responding to some puzzling questions, I realized that I was being interviewed for a job as an assistant teacher.

These stories all date from the benighted days of bigotry and discrimination before Vatican II and the women's liberation movement of the 1960s. They were among my rare encounters with such attitudes. For I was extremely fortunate. My mother, Vera Brittain, a professional writer, had confronted and then overcome her own parents' strongly held view that higher education was not for women, and that their daughter would wreck her chances of a socially successful marriage if she insisted on going to university.

My father, George Catlin, was for some years a lecturer in political science at Cornell University. His mother had been a strong supporter, before the First World War, of women's suffrage, the movement to give women the vote, a commitment so controversial that it made it almost impossible for her husband, a Church of Wales cleric, to obtain a 'living', a position as a parish priest. With such a mother, and such a wife, it was not surprising that my father brought me up from childhood to feel the full equal of my older brother. If he could climb the high bookshelves in my father's study, so could I. If he had a marshal's baton in his knapsack, so had I. The difference between our play was not particularly gender-related. My brother fought battles between his toy soldiers. I conducted elections among them.

The description of the women's revolution of the 1960s as 'the collective transformation of consciousness' is a good description. Certainly the invention of the Pill, breaking the link between sexual intercourse and procreation, was an important factor in that transformation. Furthermore, as well as the capacity to limit the size and spacing of their children, advances in maternity and health care meant that women recovered more quickly from giving birth, and lived longer active lives. More and more women lived their lives sequentially, first education and training, then paid work, then raising a family, then a return to paid work. Writers on the subject explored what they called 'Women's Two Lives'. For these women, the ponderous command that 'Anatomy is Destiny' was only partially true.[2] It is true there were not many of them. Some were seen as the exceptions that proved the rules, that women could not master 'hard sciences' like physics, that they were no good at mathematics, that they had neither the resilience nor the toughness for political leadership. But gradually example wore down the walls of prejudice.

THE DISCOVERY OF SELF-CONFIDENCE

The least explored but highly significant consequence of the women's revolution was the collective discovery of self-confidence. I call it collective, because self-confidence was built by women meeting with one another, in groups and circles, networking together, supporting one another, finding out about friendship. It may be hard to envisage now, but relations between adult women were often portrayed in the films and novels of the 1930s as bitter rivalries between women for a husband or lover. Indeed, it was argued that women were incapable of friendship. My mother wrote a sensitive book called *Testament of Friendship*, about her best friend from student days, another writer, Winifred Holtby, in repudiation of that view.

In gaining self-confidence, women also discovered their own potential. The self-doubt that had limited their aspirations, and that only the most determined had overcome, began to dissolve. In the generation that followed the 1960s, like greyhounds late out of the slips, women began to make up the lost ground. By the 1990s, in the public examinations taken by most English 16-year-olds, the so-called Ordinary Level of the General Certificate of Secondary Education (GCSE), girls outperformed boys in almost all subjects. By 2000, that was true of the Advanced Level Certificate taken at 18 (broadly the equivalent of the SAT tests), as well. And since 1999, women have outperformed men at degree level too, achieving more first class Honours degrees than their male counterparts.[3]

WOMEN AS LEADERS

Because the women's revolution and the self-confidence among women that it engendered are of relatively recent date, the highest positions of leadership in the professions and public life are still largely held by men. Given the double responsibilities that women with families bear, it is likely to remain so until there is a much more radical redistribution of family responsibilities between the sexes – an evolution that is only in its early stages. While women bear much the larger responsibility for caring for the family, both for children and for elderly parents, they are bound to bump up against a 'glass ceiling' effectively interposed by limits on the time and energy they can devote to professional life. But there have been enough women in leadership positions now to lay the old ghost of their unfitness for it, sometimes based on their alleged fragility or volatility grounded in biology.

WOMEN IN POLITICS

I remember hearing grave doubts expressed about Mrs Thatcher's capacity to be Prime Minister, based on the supposed effects on her of the menopause. Such doubts had been answered ringingly long before by the first Queen Elizabeth, who declared at the time of the Armada in 1588, 'I have the body of a weak and feeble woman, but I have the heart and stomach of a king, and a king of England too.'[4]

Similarly, women have been held to be too emotional or illogical to make independent judgements, but two women in succession, Louise Arbour and Carla del Ponte, have been appointed, on the nomination of the UN Secretary-General, Kofi Annan, to the position of Chief Prosecutor of the International Tribunal at the Hague, established to investigate war crimes and crimes against humanity in the former Yugoslavia. It is a job requiring all the tough objectivity one can imagine.

If I may be allowed a momentary lapse from benevolence, I do have to express my puzzlement that, despite the example of female Presidents in Argentina, Iceland, Ireland, the Philippines and elsewhere, and of female Prime Ministers in Bangladesh, France, India, Norway, Pakistan, Sri Lanka, Turkey, and the United Kingdom, the United States remains a patriarchal polity so far. The first US woman President is at most a gleam in someone's eye, possibly her own.

The explanation may be quite simple. One of the advantages well-educated, professional women from developing countries have is that they are not burdened by domestic responsibilities. Their position is like that of women in nineteenth-century Europe, who were supported by large domestic staffs who looked after the housework, the children, the laundry and the shopping. They have to manage, certainly, often quite a complicated operation, but they do not have to do the domestic chores themselves. Nor do they have to fund-raise for political campaigns, since most of them are scions of wealthy and respected dynasties in their own countries, which are hybrids of monarchy and democracy. Furthermore, the feminine aspect of leadership, the compassionate, all-embracing mother-figure, seems to be much more widely admired in Asia than in the macho United States.

I remember visiting India shortly after the breakaway of what was then East Pakistan to form the independent country of Bangladesh. I was engaged on a ministerial visit to the primary schools. The schoolchildren had been asked by their teachers to represent in pictures the birth of the new state. Most of them, significantly, drew the same image, of their Prime Minister, Mrs Indira Gandhi, wrapped in a substantial cloud, touching the hand of the baby Bangladesh, reminiscent of Michelangelo's image of the Creation of Man. Such a representation of Mrs Thatcher or Mrs Aquino, heads of government in Christian countries, might have been thought a little blasphemous. In India, the image evoked the pantheon of Hindu gods, which of course includes such figures as Kali and Durga, females representing aspects of the divine. How much that influences Indian voters, in an otherwise deeply gender-unequal society, I do not know. But I find it intriguing.

These women leaders have not by any means been universally impressive, wise or humble. Some have violated their own country's constitution. Some have been heavily dependent on advisors. Several are descendants of political dynasties. But in all these respects, they are not greatly different from their male counterparts. In short, it is not their biology but their individual qualities that matter, rooted within their common humanity.

'Common humanity' – a key concept easily lost in the cacophony about gender.

When I was first elected to the House of Commons in 1964, one of 29 women in a lower House of 625, women were still regarded as having a role constrained by the supposed preoccupations of their gender. Thus women ministers were usually appointed to departments concerned with health, education and pensions. Each post-war Cabinet had its single woman member, known as 'the statutory woman'. In the United States, not every post-war administration had a woman in the Cabinet. Of the four who were so appointed prior to President Clinton's election in 1992, two were Secretaries of Labor. Roosevelt appointed Frances Perkins to the job in 1932, and George Bush appointed Lynn Martin in 1990.

It was not until the advent of Harold Wilson as Prime Minister of the United Kingdom in 1964 that women in the UK were appointed to a whole range of ministerial jobs not usually associated with feminine preoccupations – transport, overseas aid, prisons, economic affairs, foreign affairs and Northern Ireland. Wilson was not influenced by a person's gender in making his choices. And he was borne out; the women did as well in the 'masculine' jobs as in the 'feminine' ones. But the most significant impact of women on public life has not been their individual contributions. It has been the radical change in the agenda of politics.

Before women had votes, and before they could be elected as MPs or Representatives, the agenda of politics was dominated by issues of power – foreign policy, national security, the military and finance. By the inter-war years, the politics of welfare had become important – pensions, education, health, housing; by the post-war years, at least in Europe, they had become central. Parties in Europe vied to construct family-friendly policies, starting with child allowances and moving on to provision for maternity leave and flexible working hours to help the growing army of working mothers. Christian Democrats and Social Democrats alike were convinced that the state had an obligation to help families, in particular those with low incomes, through the tax system and through social legislation.

But the influence of women on the political agenda went deeper still, not only in Europe but elsewhere, including North America. Political attitudes towards conflict situations began to move away from the patriarchal code of retribution, revenge and punishment, towards a more inclusive ethic of consensus, reconciliation and respect for human rights. Among the countries advocating this new approach were the Scandinavians, where women held a large number of political positions. Among those practising it was contemporary South Africa, where women played a crucial role in the transition from apartheid to democracy. Observers of that difficult but ultimately successful process have paid tribute to the determination of the women to reach solutions by patient negotiation, eschewing any resort to violence.

CATHOLIC STEREOTYPES

How strange, then, that the Church that advocates these values so strongly – forgiveness, reconciliation, peace and subsidiarity, the making of decisions at the lowest level consonant with efficacy – has found so little room for women within its structures. On his remarkable missionary journeys, the Pope has stressed the centrality of human rights, sought to bring antagonists together, excoriated violence, asked for and offered forgiveness. He has opposed wars and condemned capital punishment and has pleaded for justice for the world's poor, of whom the majority are women. But neither shared beliefs and commitments nor proven ability seem able to alter the stereotypical view of women held by the bureaucrats of the Vatican.

Those stereotypes are long cherished. One is modelled on the Virgin Mary, gentle, pure and humble, obedient to the will of God, yet so loving that she acts as an intermediary for the whole suffering and sinful human race. The other is Eve, seductive and defiant, tempting Adam to abandon Paradise. Neither is recognizable as a full human being, unlike the women in the New Testament, who of course include Mary as Mother of God. They relate directly to Jesus, talking with Him as a friend, learning from Him and, in the case of Mary Magdalen and other women disciples, bearing witness to His Resurrection.

The advantage of a stereotype is that it obviates the need to come to terms with another human being – another being made in the image of God. And this is what the Vatican has found it difficult to do. For what must be understood is not the femininity of women, but their humanity, their right to the dignity and respect accorded to all the children of God.

This is where the importance of dialogue with the laity enters the scene, the laity of whom *Lumen Gentium* declared:

> The joys and the hopes, the griefs and the anxieties of the people of this age, especially those who are poor or in any way afflicted, these too are the joys and hopes, the griefs and anxieties of the followers of Christ. Indeed nothing genuinely human fails to raise an echo in their hearts. For theirs is a community composed of people. United in Christ, they are led by the Holy Spirit in their journey to the Kingdom of their Father and they have welcomed the news of salvation which is meant for everyone. That is why the community realises that it is truly and intimately connected with humankind and its history.[5]

The words of *Lumen Gentium* are inspiring, but how can a celibate clergy understand what the forbidding of artificial contraception in *Humanae Vitae* means for a married woman? How can they weigh the strains on marriage of abstaining from lovemaking, possibly for years, because to make love would risk the health of the mother or the economic viability of the family? And how do they respond to defending a doctrine expressed in *Humanae Vitae* that was rejected by a clear majority of a Vatican-appointed Commission in the 1960s, whose recommendations were overturned by a liberal Pope, Paul VI, because he could not bring himself to negate the pronouncements of his predecessors? Today his Commission's recommendations are followed by 80 per cent of the Church's lay people, an ironic statement of the *sensus fidelium*. If the Vatican was minded to discuss such issues openly with the laity, allowing for the range of opinions held among them, some of the tragic mistakes and misunderstandings of the years since the Second Vatican Council concluded might well have been avoided.

When I was a young woman, I belonged to St Joan's Alliance, a Catholic organization, one of whose aims was the ordination of women. The organization was regarded quite benevolently by the Church, and no one ever told me that I should not belong. Today the question of women's ordination has become more fraught, perhaps because Rome is much more troubled than it was then about the place of women in the Church. The Anglican Church now accepts the ordination of women, and has a steady stream of women choosing the vocation of the priesthood. In consequence of the bitter reaction among some Anglicans to that radical innovation, the Roman Catholic Church accepted married priests of the Church of England who have abandoned their Church for Roman Catholicism as being validly ordained, and has not required them to revoke their marriage vows.[6] So some compromise with a strictly celibate priesthood seems possible, if only because so many priests have abandoned their vocation owing to the commitment to celibacy it entails. I am in no position to offer an authoritative or definitive view on the theological aspects of the question. But I find the prohibition on even *discussing* the possibility of women's ordination very hard to accept.

What I can say, even as a lay person, is that there are a number of influential positions in the Church that are not sacerdotal and are therefore not restricted to men in principle, only in practice. Any serious resumption of the dialogue with the laity would give women an opportunity to contribute to discussion on the contemporary mission of the Church. Already, distinguished women hold senior academic posts as professors of theology or of scripture. In recognition of the fundamental importance of women to the Church, the Vatican might set up a Commission on the role of women within it. It could not do better in launching such a Commission than the announcement of significant appointments of leading Catholic women to the Church's administration. For us women, who are the disenfranchised faithful, such a gesture of belief in our humanity and our ability would come none too soon.

NOTES

1. *The Culture of Life* (London: Catholic Institute for International Relations, 2000), ISBN 1852872330.
2. Sigmund Freud, *Collected Works* (1924), Vol. 5.
3. Department for Education and Skills, UK, 2002.
4. Queen Elizabeth I addressing the troops at Tilbury on the approach of the Armada, 1588.

5. Abbott, W. M., SJ (ed.), *Pastoral Constitution on the Church in the Modern World*, from *The Documents of Vatican II* (New York: Guild Press, 1966), pp. 299–300.

6. The Catholic church continues to demand celibacy from those Anglican priests *not* already married who want to become Catholic priests.

Chapter 4

The Political Vocation

In the 'Pastoral Constitution on the Church in the Modern World', *Gaudium et Spes*, the Second Vatican Council called upon Christians to take an active part in the life of society. 'We can justly consider,' the Council wrote, 'that the future of humanity lies in the hands of those who are strong enough to provide coming generations with reasons for living and hoping'. In a much more recent document, *The Common Good*, a statement by the Catholic Bishops' Conference of England and Wales produced shortly before the General Election of 1997, the message is stated more explicitly: 'we particularly wish to declare our respect and gratitude towards all those who undertake the responsibilities of political life, whatever party they belong to'; and 'Politics is an honourable vocation, which often exacts great personal cost from those who engage in it, and from their families.'[1]

I am walking down a row of houses in a small town in England's Lake District. I knock on the door of one of them. 'No, I'm not going to vote', the householder tells me. 'They're all the same. They're just in it for what they can get out of it.'

I am replying to a phone-in election programme on the BBC. A lady calling in tells me she is not going to vote. 'I'm utterly disillusioned,' she says. 'They never say what they mean, or mean what they say.' To her surprise, I argue with her.

I am disillusioned, too. After all, I have been criss-crossing the country for days on end, by train and plane and car, talking to voters, trying to explain our policies to them. No one pays me to do this. I am not even running for a seat myself. I could just sit at home, or take off for a holiday in Italy or Greece. And here I am being abused for taking part in the political process, because I believe in democracy and I believe in the policies my party is putting forward.

Such attitudes to politicians are by no means unique to the United Kingdom. I used to teach every year at the Kennedy School of Government in Harvard a class entitled 'To Be a Politician', intended for young men and women who felt they had a political vocation: I have mentioned it already. The course was named after a rousing book by an author called Stimson Bullitt, who had never been successful, but had an astonishing insight into the vocation of politics. A year or so after I had started the course, some of the students came to see me. 'Do you think you could change the name of this course?' they inquired. 'Maybe something like "The American Political Process"?' 'But that's both dreary and abstract,' I riposted. 'What's the point?' It took me a little while to realize that my students felt their attendance at a course with so explicit an intention would damage their career prospects, would not look good among the list of course credits. The suspicion of politics out there, I realized, was serious.

How do I reconcile these two things, the measured statements of the bishops and the dismissive response of some of the voters? Part of the explanation lies in something I wrote about in my second chapter, the death of deference. 'The Member of Parliament (or Congressman) is no better than I am. Why should I defer to him? He's not better educated. He probably doesn't even earn as much.'

Then there is another part to the explanation, the media crusade to investigate every public figure, not only his present but his past, for any flaws or lapses. I wrote about that too in my second chapter. That crusade is sustained by political consultants employed by the parties, one of whose jobs is to dig out material for negative broadcasts, ammunition in the unending party battles that typify the adversarial political system. 'I've read all about sleaze in the newspapers. He's probably got his hand in the till, like all the rest of them.'

So you, the politician, start out with two strikes against you. You are entering one of the least respected professions. Everything you do, at least if you are in national or state politics, will be closely monitored. You will have to work long hours, and be responsive to crises or personal appeals for help at any time of the day or night. You will have to respond to scores, even hundreds, of e-mails and letters every week, some of them about complicated matters that cannot be answered routinely, some of them highly offensive. Most weekends, you will be in your constituency conducting advice sessions, opening fêtes, addressing voluntary organizations and being criticized at local party meetings.

So why do it? Well, there are huge compensations. One is the excitement of being at the ringside seat of great events. On these occasions, the House of Commons, which is much more of a debating chamber than the House of Representatives, let alone the Senate, pulses with life. Television gives a bit of that sense of excitement to everyone, but it is not quite the same. The viewer is an observer, not a participant. Even in everyday matters, there is still the satisfaction of explaining one's position well, or scoring an effective point.

Then there is the belief that one might be able to sway decisions or influence policies even in a small way. There is the satisfaction of winning a case for a constituent, or amending a bill in a way that may help hundreds, even thousands of people. There is the collegiality of being a member of a party combining together for a particular objective in which it believes. And, from time to time, there is the sense of a great moral issue where you are on the right side.

Politics is sometimes reduced in modern parlance to management. The political choice is about which party can manage the economy better. That is a legitimate issue, but to reduce politics to its economic dimension only is to make it about less than what is fully human. Politics, as I pointed out earlier, is bound up with the making of moral choices, and it is a great illusion to suppose that economics is somehow inviolate and morally autonomous, that the market makes the choices so we should not have to.

MORAL CHOICES IN POLITICS

Let me offer some illustrations of these moral choices in politics – not to argue the rightness of one side or the other, though I know where I stand on each of them, but because all of them involve values about which Christians themselves often disagree.

My mother once wrote to the tax inspectors to say that she had been undertaxed. At the time, tax rates on higher incomes in Britain were well over 80 per cent. She regarded the payment of taxes as a civic duty. And here is one of the moral choices politicians and citizens are called upon to make. It is an issue that deeply divides Christians. Some believe that high taxation discourages individual enterprise, and enables the state to extend its power over individuals. A low-tax state will be a high-growth state, and in the end that will, they believe, improve society's prosperity and therefore, by trickle-down, the prospects of the poor.

Other Christians argue that society has an obligation to the poor and needy, the old and the sick, which requires the provision of public services paid for by the state – or, in other words, the taxpayers. The principle evoked here is that of solidarity, the inclusion of everyone in society. It has been an important driving force behind the so-called 'social market' that still prevails in Europe, a free market curbed and regulated to conform to social goals.

The received opinion of pollsters has long been that any pledge to increase personal taxes is electorally disastrous. Do you remember George Bush, senior –'read my lips, no new taxes'? But, in the United Kingdom, the party advocating tax cuts was comprehensively defeated in the election of 2001, and the one advocating tax increases improved its position. The electorate seems willing to pay the taxes needed for the public services it wants to see.

Capital punishment is another moral issue to challenge politicians. In the United States, the Supreme Court has an important role in determining the constitutionality of this ultimate punishment, but it has in recent years by and large chosen not to intervene in individual states' use of the death penalty. In 1976, the Supreme Court gave the green light to states with the death penalty to recommence executions following a four-year moratorium, during which the Supreme Court had required the rewriting of statutes providing for capital murder offences.[2] The Court had ruled that Georgia's legislation, as then written, potentially provided for the imposition of a 'cruel and unusual punishment' and was thus unconstitutional.

But the way was open for the use of the death penalty again, with carefully rewritten statutes. It began in Utah, with the execution of Gary Gilmore, who had asked to die. In the following 24 years, the numbers executed have risen dramatically, with the emphasis on certain southern states. From one execution in 1977 in the entire United States, former Governor Bush of Texas, now the American President, approved the execution of over 130 convicts in that state alone during his five years in office. This has reflected public opinion in the United States, which throughout most of the period overwhelmingly supported the use of capital punishment.

That support has begun to wane as concern has arisen over both the deterrence value of state executions (the average homicide rate is slightly higher in death penalty states, at 9.3 per 100,000 inhabitants, than for the United States as a whole, which is 9 per 100,000[3]) and the fear that innocent people may have been executed. The Governor of Illinois placed a moratorium on executions after discovering that thirteen of its Death Row inmates had been wrongly convicted, while an equivalent number had been put to death, some of whose cases raise similar doubts. The state's Governor, George Ryan, commuted all outstanding death sentences shortly prior to retiring from office.[4] Concerns of this kind had put an end to the death penalty in Europe much earlier. In the United Kingdom, at least, it is true to say that this was due to Parliament overriding public opinion.

Revulsion in Europe against the death penalty was so strong that its abolition became one of the benchmarks of fitness for membership of the European Union. Capital punishment has now been officially abolished throughout the Union, with the strong support of the Vatican. Internationally and nationally, the issue divides Christians. That division is not based on a pragmatic study of the deterrent effect of capital punishment. It reflects, rather, deep differences in moral values.

Abortion is disapproved of by most Christians and many members of other religions too. In practice, what happens is affected not only by moral values but by the nature of political systems. In the United States, the legality or otherwise of abortion depends upon the verdict of the Supreme Court, whether or not the *Roe* v. *Wade* decision will be overturned. Passionate interests are lined up on either side. In most European countries, the issue is one for Parliament, not the courts, and in pluralist legislatures in which no one party has a majority, the tendency is to settle on a compromise, liked by none but bearable by most. In the United Kingdom, that compromise was for easy abortion in the first trimester of pregnancy, and an almost complete ban on abortion in the final trimester, with the dividing point falling in the second trimester on medical grounds, influenced by the stage at which a foetus is capable of surviving if delivered, a borderline pushed downwards as medical science advances. This is, of course, an instance of the triumph of relativism. All one can say in its favour is that the horror of partial birth abortion is forbidden by law.

Where political issues involve matters of conscience, and therefore party directions on how to vote are considered inappropriate, it is in the nature of parliaments to try to reach compromises, if only to avoid embarrassing colleagues.

I remember well in the discussion preceding the debates on the 1967 Abortion Bill how a number of us, Catholic MPs, suggested to the bishops that we would get more support if the Vatican made a sharp distinction between contraception and abortion in the hierarchy of sins. We needed to attract Anglican support to impose stronger limits on legalized abortion, but the Anglicans were unsympathetic to the Catholic view of birth control. Not unreasonably, they argued that contraception was a much less objectionable way of limiting family size than abortion, but that the Catholic position, making no such distinction, was driving parents to get rid of the unborn babies they did not want or could not care for. Pope Paul VI's encylical, *Humanae Vitae*, we felt, repeating the Vatican's total opposition to artificial birth control, isolated us even more from the mainstream of Christian, let alone broader public, opinion.

I mentioned earlier that once in a while some great public issue comes along that dominates political life for a long time, so majestic the moral issues involved, so difficult and portentous the decisions to be made. Such issues divide societies and political parties, and may even split families and set brother against sister. Such an issue was slavery. Slavery troubled the Papacy centuries before it split the United States. While there were few slaves in Europe, as distinct from serfs tied to their master's land, the founding of empires abroad by Spain and Portugal, and later by Britain and France, led to the institution of slavery, as the indigenous inhabitants were forced to serve on the planta- tions and in the mines controlled by their foreign conquerors.

The Vatican has been bitterly criticized over the years for compromising on this issue because it was financially beholden to the great Iberian kingdoms. Recent historical research shows this criticism to be unjust. In 1435, Pope Eugene IV protested against the capturing of natives of the Canary Islands for slavery. He ordered those engaged in the trade to 'restore to their earlier liberty all and each person of either sex' on pain of excommunication.[5] On 20 March 1686, the Holy Office, moved by reports from a leading envoy of the black confraternities, Lourenco da Silva, and by a damning report of the slave trade in the Congo from Capuchin missionaries, denounced the whole spectrum of abuses connected with slavery.[6] 'Unjust slavery' and 'racial slavery' were seen by the Papacy as different in principle from using prisoners or hostages of war in that capacity. What particularly appalled the Holy Office was the concept of perpetual slavery, slavery as a category from which a human being could not be rescued. In his 1839 decree, Pope Gregory XVI described the slave traders as men 'shamefully blinded by the desire of sordid gain' who 'did not hesitate to reduce to slavery Indians, blacks and other unfortunate peoples'. Leo XIII urged the Brazilian bishops to work for the abolition of slavery there. Over the years, the Popes consistently denounced slavery, in terms that call to mind some of the campaigns of human rights advocates today. The difficulty was that local officials, ecclesiastical and secular alike, their careers dependent upon pleasing monarchs and sometimes local bishops, were extremely reluctant to do anything about it. As with the present Holy Father's preaching on poverty, there was no lack of papal leadership; rather there was a deliberate deafness among those able to implement what the Vatican demanded.

Such a fateful issue for me has been the construction of the European Union, and British membership of it. Bringing together proud and ancient nation states to pool their sovereignty in a common market, a common commitment to the protection of the environment, a common code of human rights and a supranational supreme court, is a controversial and fraught endeavour. It is even harder than forging the United States out of its quarrelsome separate elements, and that needed the genius of the Founding Fathers. For the nationalist sentiments of European states are long rooted in histories of conflict.

The cause of an integrated Europe has shaped my whole political life, and there is still a long way to go. But already huge progress has been made towards two great goals. War among the Union's fifteen member states is now unthinkable. Yet all through the past centuries, they have fought one another. Their commitment now, in law if not always in practice, is to what the Second Vatican Council called 'the common good'.

To grasp the scale of this achievement, the substitution of the politics of negotiation and peace for the violence of war, consider just for a moment the scale of the human and material losses of the two world wars of the last century, which were in essence European civil wars. Both began in Europe and then dragged in the United States, Asia and Africa, by way of alliances and imperial or Commonwealth connections. Tens of millions died, or were gravely wounded, often experiencing unspeakable agony. Whole cities, some of them among humanity's highest cultural achievements, were devastated or destroyed. The wealth of what was, in 1914, the world's richest continent was dissipated in the buying of arms. And the thirst for revenge that drove the victors after the First World War to impose on the defeated Germans the Treaty of Versailles engendered in its turn the ferocious nationalism that led to the resumption of the war in 1939, engulfing a new generation.

The cost of the wars went beyond even the terrible losses of human lives and material resources. The warrior's code, crude though it was, that protected unarmed civilians and in particular women and children, that saw war as a conflict between armed men, collapsed before the doctrine of total war, where any method that might break the morale of the other side was condoned. The destruction of Guernica in 1937 by Nazi bombers during the civil war in Spain, immortalized by Pablo Picasso in his terrifying painting, was the first such incident. It was to be followed by an escalation of attacks on civilians, first the Blitz in London, then the mass bombing of Germany, finally the destruction of Hiroshima and Nagasaki by atomic bombs. Such a dramatic departure from civilized norms was, it was argued, justified by the absolute necessity to destroy the cancer of Nazism, which had systematically annihilated so many of the people, Jewish and non-Jewish, within its power.

Faced with the rabid nationalism of Fascism, and terrified of the onward march of atheistic Communism, the Christian churches had wavered in the years between the wars. In Germany, the Protestant churches, with some noble individual exceptions like the pastor Dietrich Bonhoeffer, threw in their lot with the National Socialist government. Roman Catholics, both in Germany and Italy, began by condemning the new totalitarianism. The centre political parties, mainly supported by Catholics, fought strongly against the destruction of their democracies. But those centre parties could not count on the support of the Vatican, pursuing its own policy of making treaties, known as concordats, with the dictators. John Cornwell in his profoundly troubling biography of Pope Pius XII, *Hitler's Pope*, presents a highly partisan account, accusing the Vatican of deliberately undermining the Centre Party of Germany to reach its concordat with Hitler.[7]

It is clear from contemporary documents that Pope Pius XI, and his Secretary of State, Eugenio Pacelli, the future Pope Pius XII, had no liking for the Nazis and detested their racialism.[8] Pope Pius XI was robust in his denunciation of Nazism, culminating in his encyclical of 1937, *Mit Brennende Sorge*. Knowing that the price of any Vatican denunciations of Nazism would be paid for by the deportations and deaths of ordinary good German Catholics and their priests, it was perhaps understandable that his successor, Pope Pius XII, was so cautious. So the Vatican tried to make its peace with the totalitarians, through concordats intended to protect the position of the Roman Catholic Church. Looking back, the silence of Pius XII's

Vatican, as Jews, Gypsies and others were rounded up, beaten and systematically destroyed, must count as one of the more shameful periods in the long history of the Church, partly redeemed by the deaths of many defiant priests in Nazi concentration camps.

The excuse is that Communism was seen at the time as a much more dangerous adversary by the Church, which could not afford to antagonize the extreme Right while defending itself against the extreme Left. For Pope Pius XII, evidently a deeply devout and scholarly man, the dilemma must have been acute. But faced with such evidence of evil, was there no more, by personal action or gesture, he could have done to condemn it?

The descent into moral nihilism affected my own family, and is one reason for my distrust of nationalism, my commitment to international institutions and, in particular, to the European Union as a way station towards a new moral order. My mother, whose fiancé, only brother and best friends had all been killed in the First World War, had become a pacifist renouncing war whatever the purpose. In 1944, when she learned through the witness of bishops in neutral Sweden, confirmed by Bishop Bell, the Anglican Bishop of Chichester, that German cities were being systematically destroyed by what was called 'carpet bombing', in which hundreds of thousands of civilians were burned and suffocated to death, conscience drove her to make a public protest. She wrote a pamphlet called *Massacre by Bombing* which was published by the Fellowship of Reconciliation, a small Christian group. The pamphlet pleaded with the Allies to stop mass bombing.[9]

The pamphlet elicited an extraordinary reaction. It was denounced by President Roosevelt and in the House of Commons. Bishops thundered against it from their pulpits.

Only a tiny brave minority, including the Quakers, Bishop George Bell of Chichester, and in the United States a handful of Protestant ministers and Dorothy Day's Catholic Workers' Movement, stood their ground.

Emerging from this most terrible of wars, a generation of European politicians whose countries had been conquered, invaded and sacked, determined it should never happen again and turned from revenge to the politics of reconciliation. In this they were supported, encouraged and led by the United States. The Marshall Plan, unprecedented in international politics, was described by Winston Churchill, Britain's wartime Prime Minister, as 'the most unsordid act in history'. It was the foundation for the building of the European Community.

Fifty years on from the signing of the Treaty of Paris, the first step towards a common market in coal and steel, a new moral order began slowly to emerge, based not on war but on respect for human rights and on the rule of law. The European Convention on Human Rights, like the UN Declaration on Human Rights and the Inter-American Charter, dates back to the post-war years, having been drawn up in 1950. The European Court of Human Rights was set up to judge cases brought by individual petitioners against states which they claimed had abused those rights.

Now most European countries have incorporated the Convention into their own domestic law, making redress for individuals much faster and much less expensive. No legislation can be introduced in these countries without a statement being made by the minister responsible, for which he or she is accountable in law, that the proposed legislation is compatible with the Convention. And now no nation can aspire to join the European Union unless it satisfies the existing members that it will respect human rights within its own national jurisdiction.

There is a parallel evolution in establishing limits to national behaviour on a worldwide basis. The war crimes tribunals in Rwanda, Yugoslavia and elsewhere grew out of horror that such atrocities could still happen, and guilt that the developed world had not tried to stop them. Television and radio, the unsilenced accusers, do not allow the rest of us to conceal or forget what happened, as we used to. Nor can the developed world act after the fact. The mass media show what is happening as it occurs, and we cannot pretend ignorance.

It was television and radio that precipitated the NATO intervention in Kosovo. The ethnic cleansing of the Kosovo Albanians was of course denied by the government of Yugoslavia. What was happening, they claimed, was the suppression of terrorism. But the evidence accumulated. I spent a week there in January 1999, seeing villages put to the torch, hearing the crump of mortars and the staccato of machine-guns directed at villages and the inhabitants huddled within them.

The world's only global political instrument, the United Nations, is of course subject to a veto by any permanent member of the Security Council, and there was no consensus among its members on intervening. Indeed, a Russian veto was highly likely. So the intervention was undertaken by NATO at best on shaky legal ground. Retrospectively, however, the evidence to justify that intervention is being painstakingly put together by the investigators of the War Crimes Tribunal at the Hague. The mass graves of Croatia, Bosnia and Kosovo are telling their own grim stories.

The next step in this slow evolution towards a world of law based on a shared moral code is the International Criminal Court, able to look into the abuse of human rights anywhere in the world, and whichever nations are involved. The treaty establishing the Court had, as of January 2003, been ratified by 87 countries, and has come into force. But it is being vigorously contested by the world's most powerful country, the United States, which is bringing immense pressure to bear on its friends and allies to enter into bilateral treaties committing themselves in no circumstances to hand over American citizens for trial by the Court. If the United States succeeds, other nations may insist upon special treatment and the Court's credibility will be undermined.

The steps already taken to construct an international legal and moral code are encouraging – except that this majestic structure means nothing in those parts of the world that are consigned to poverty, hunger, disease and war. Such countries, many of them failed or failing states, are engaged in the most brutal battles for survival in territories where there are not enough resources of food, land and water to go round, where life, in Hobbes's phrase, is 'nasty, brutish, and short'. The Church, being universal, has insisted on drawing our attention to these human hells.

NOTES

1. *The Common Good and the Catholic Church's Social Teaching*, the Catholic Bishops' Conference of England and Wales, 1996.
2. The green light was given in the Supreme Court ruling of 2 July 1976.
3. According to *Scientific American*, February 2001.
4. Announced by Governor Ryan on 11 January 2003, at Northwestern University College of Law, USA.
5. Pope Eugene IV in 1435 wrote to Bishop Ferdinand of Lanzarote in his Bull, *Sicut Dudum*.
6. On 20 March 1686, the Holy Office of the Holy See condemned the abuses of the Atlantic slave trade. The violent and fraudulent enslavement of 'Negroes and other natives' was forbidden, and owners were to emancipate and compensate innocent slaves.

7.   John Cornwell, *Hitler's Pope: The Secret History of Pius XII* (London: Viking, 1999).

8.   Jose M. Sanchez, *Pius XII and the Holocaust: Understanding the Controversy* (Washington DC: Catholic University of America Press, 2002).

9.   Vera Brittain, *Seed of Chaos: What Mass Bombing Really Means* (London: New Vision Publishing Co., 1944). Published in the USA as *Massacre by Bombing: The Facts Behind The British–American Attack On Germany* (Nyack: Fellowship, 1944).

Chapter 5

The Gospel to the Poor

Globalization has become the term widely used to describe a number of phenomena characteristic of our times. It helps to distinguish between the strands of the idea, if only to enable it to be discussed clearly. Firstly, globalization describes a technological revolution based on almost universal access to television, on the Internet and on the spread of information technology to a very large part of the world, and in particular to the educated members of most societies – in short, interconnectedness worldwide. The technological revolution also has its analogue in the ease and speed of physical communications, by telephone, simple and cheap air travel and private car.

Technological advances have been complemented by significant institutional changes responding to the global reach of trade in both goods and services. The General Agreement on Tariffs and Trade (GATT), which itself brought about substantial reductions in tariffs, has been succeeded by the World Trade Organization, whose dispute procedures are binding on member states, thereby over-riding national sovereign rights. Under its aegis, the reduction of protective barriers has been taken further, and now applies to services as well as goods, and even to intellectual property.

THE GLOBAL CUSTOMER

The globalization of the market is not driven only by multinational corporations, of which there are now over 60,000. It is also driven by consumer choice. Consumers have happily embraced the globalization of the market for goods. They look for fresh fruit and vegetables year round, often entailing long journeys for such commodities by air from Africa or Latin America.

They have become eclectic in their tastes for exotic cuisines and ethnic clothes. Everywhere the best products of the world are marketed to those with the money to indulge their tastes, a global Ali Baba's cave. The global market extends too to cultural products, though the market for them is more limited because of the barriers of language – films, books, contemporary art. The hunger for roots, for old, secure communities, drives consumers to search for local crafts and customs recalling them to a different and more settled age.

Globalization, for all that it is at the centre of fierce controversy, is not itself a moral force. It describes a social and economic phenomenon with which we are all familiar. How it affects real people in the real world depends upon its interaction with the political, legal and cultural framework of the societies they live in, and on the values and attitudes of the individuals engaged with it. How it operates and how it impinges on people are not, therefore, morally neutral. Nor are they inevitable.

MANAGING GLOBALIZATION

Responses to globalization tell us a lot about the limitations of economics. Early analysts welcomed the phenomenon since it increased competition, promised a more efficient use of resources and opened up new markets. It seemed to be conducive to growth, which was the main objective of international economic institutions, and the key to improved standards of living. What has subsequently emerged, however, from the tribulations of the last twenty years, is that globalization without good government and accountable institutions can be a high road to the social and economic polarization of populations, massive corruption and environmental degradation. Protesters who rage against globalization are spitting into the wind; it is its operation in practice that should animate them.

Adam Smith's market operated to produce the best outcome for all those engaged in commerce, by way of enlightened self-interest and freedom of choice. It was that rare thing, a near perfect market, where all alike enjoyed equal access and equal information. Smith lived in an unusually stable and enlightened society, late eighteenth-century Edinburgh, with its strong civic sense, its commitment to education and its high moral standards. These attributes were taken as given; there was no need to raise questions about good governance or individual responsibility. Much could be taken on trust. Smith's market was a market of equals, suppliers and consumers both seeking the best outcome for themselves, but within the limits provided by a strong social framework.

In most markets, in practice, differences of power hugely distort competition. Powerful producers may dominate a market, or even achieve a monopoly. Powerful consumers – supermarkets provide a good contemporary example – may negotiate better deals at lower prices than the market offers to small shopkeepers or individuals. Furthermore, access to information, and the ability to understand that information, varies greatly between consumers. Where information is controlled or patchy, those who possess it gain substantial advantage. That is obviously true in societies where information is controlled and large areas of secrecy obtain.

In some societies, what matters most in commerce is whom you know or to whom you may be related. All of us are familiar with situations where one is told, 'It's no use bidding for that. The state/council is certain to give it to x.' This is a mild form of the corruption endemic in certain societies where free markets do not operate, and where commerce can only be activated or contracts signed by members of the ruling families, or after the payment of a bribe.

THE INFORMED CONSUMER

I had a riveting example of how imperfect markets are in my own professional life. My first post at Cabinet level was a peculiarly awful one, guaranteed to entrap even the most cautious office-bearer. I became Secretary of State for Prices and Consumer Protection in March 1974, during a period of rapid inflation, driven in part by the massive increases in oil prices in 1973. There was not much I could do about it, but clearly as a minister in a democratically elected government, I had to try and be seen to try. I experimented with a lot of things, a complex system of price restraints, cross-subsidization of necessities by higher prices for luxuries and so on. None of these measures was popular with the companies with which I had to deal. Curiously, however, the policy that attracted much the most angry resistance was not one of regulation or control, but my decision to list publicly in the local newspapers or on placards in front of the town halls the prices of the most heavily bought goods and where they could be obtained. Here were the core facts of competition, readily obtainable by all, just as Adam Smith would have wished. And here, too, was an acute awareness that information, even of this simple kind, would go far to destroy the imperfections on which the sellers depended for their profit.

NO FREE MARKET HERE

The global market is deeply imperfect, not only because limits on information are magnified by differences of language, taste and culture, but because it offers no freedom to trade in the case of the one factor of production most readily available to the poor, labour – the work of one's mind or hands. The eager student of Adam Smith who lives in Mexico or Indonesia will encounter free, or at least relatively free, trade in goods and services, and freedom of capital, that most fungible of factors. But if, as a true aficionado of neo-liberalism, s/he decides to sell his or her labour on a global free market, s/he will immediately run into difficulty. Unless possessed of skills that are in demand, s/he is unlikely to be allowed to sell the only commodity he or she has. He may try to enter another country illegally, but he may risk his health and even his life in the effort.

Locked into a country with little demand for what he can offer, he must either sell his labour at a much lower price than he could command in the global market, or go hungry. The adamant refusal of the rich countries to accept free movement of labour – and far from lowering with globalization, the barriers go up higher and higher – means that the playing field of global trade is far from level. If labour could move around readily, the wages of the developing world would rise, and those of the developed world fall dramatically. But the free market is free only for the rich and powerful; for the poor in poor countries, it is a sham.

THE CALL FOR SOCIAL JUSTICE

Let me break off here to tell you a true story, the story of a challenge to this unjust economic system, a system in which traditional structures of power distort the working of the market. So great were those distortions that the challengers described them as 'structures of sin'. The place was Latin America. The challengers were Catholic bishops and priests and an aroused laity, the faithful 'people of God'. Their radical message was the Gospel of Jesus Christ, applied to the experience of the contemporary world. They called it 'liberation theology'.

It was, I recall, a handsome, rather pretentious hotel with white balconies, heavy wooden doors with golden knobs and creased bellboys standing at attention behind them, a garden rioting with orange lilies and scarlet bougainvillea surrounded by a wall. Beyond the wall, a fast road ran between the hotel and the shining beaches of Ipanema, one of the most luxurious neighbourhoods of Rio de Janeiro.

I was there for the party that preceded the conference of a prestigious American organization concerned with international relations. Among its honoured guests was Dr Henry Kissinger. Important people strolled around the garden bearing exotic cocktails, smiling and assessing one another's status. In the sky, a few birds contended with a distant helicopter lazily patrolling the scene. And then there was an explosion, a sudden yellow flare of fire and a thud as part of the wall collapsed. Within seconds, security guards had leaped into the gap, police sirens were shrieking and Dr Kissinger was spirited away. The date was 1984, but in many ways it was a G7 sort of occasion, right down to the discovery that four joyriding youngsters had crashed their extremely expensive sports car into the wall by accident, killing three of the occupants in the process. Beautiful, rich, crazy Brazil.

THE GOSPEL TO THE POOR

It is a few days later, and I am walking up a pile of earth and rubble scooped out of the ground for the construction of a new highway in Belo Horizonte, Brazil. Already, under the bridge that will lift the highway across a valley, dozens of Brazilian families have made homes for themselves out of petrol tins, planks and bits of wood and plastic. One home boasts a colour television but no proper roof or walls. The luxuries these people do not have are water and sewage systems. Dead animals, bits of candy papers, vegetable stalks and human faeces mingle in the ditches that run through the barrio.

Today, however, is an auspicious day. Sister Teresa, the energetic little nun who lives among the barrio dwellers, laid claim to the pile of earth and the road-makers were willing to yield it up. The pile is being sifted for stones, and planted with beans and corn. Sister Teresa thinks forty, maybe fifty families can live off the pile. As she walks purposefully among the little plants, gesturing for water here or terracing there, she sweeps one dusty toddler after another into her arms, hugging them and then putting them down to make room for the next. Hers is a voyage of love.

That night, in the mission, the young seminarians, a spectrum from white to black, sit on the stoop in the velvet evening, playing guitars and singing hymns and folk songs. Beyond the circle of firelight, the eyes of children stud the darkness. The little community seems to hug itself.

The next day, Sunday, I see more clearly what binds them together. The head of the mission, an Irish priest of the Order of the Divine Word, takes me to the first of several

Masses, one or two outdoors, one in a little wooden church. They are crowded, the congregations taking vigorous part in the singing, occasionally interrupting the sermons, one of which is delivered with great passion by a woman community leader. It is about the Gospel to the poor, and is replete with quotations from the New Testament, especially the Beatitudes and the parables of Jesus walking, eating with and caring for the poor. The worshippers are evidently familiar with the New Testament. The Scriptures speak to them now, about their current condition, about their sense of the world's injustice, about their dreams of a better life. The words of Jesus are electric with meaning.

These men and women belong to one of the *comunidades de base*, the Bible study groups that are the building blocks of liberation theology. The poor have been heard, and out of their pain has come a new and vibrant life. We are, they feel, the children of God. We have regained our dignity. Our Church has at long last listened to us. Up in Recife, in the north-east, a province so desperate children beg from every passing car, Bishop Hélder Câmara is helping the poor and the landless discover their own potential, creating communities that help one another. Down in São Paulo, Cardinal Arns is challenging the complacent rich of his diocese, reminding them of the obligations Christians have to the poor. One businessman satirizes the Cardinal to me: 'He is like a melon,' the man tells me, 'Green outside and pink within.'

'Pink within.' The businessman captures the suspicion conservative lay people share with conservative clerics. Liberation theology is revolutionary, radical; maybe it is first cousin to Communism. Certainly it challenges the distribution of land and wealth in Latin America; certainly it asks whether so great a gap between rich and poor can be condoned by Christians. In Brazil, where today the richest fifth of the population enjoys twenty-nine times the income of the poorest fifth, it is a very relevant question.[1]

Liberation theology, like a tropical flower, burst upon the Latin American scene in the early 1960s. Some of its early apostles were Franciscan priests from Petropolis, the theological seminary near Rio de Janeiro, in particular Father Leonardo Boff and the Brazilian Jesuit Father Joao Batista Libanio. The first exponent of the thesis was the Dominican Father Gustavo Gutiérrez, now a professor at the University of Notre Dame in the United States.

Many events contributed to the huge impact of liberation theology in Latin America – the successful revolution in Cuba, the liberation of former colonies in Africa and Asia in the 1960s, the radical mood of the 1960s, the formidable challenge of Soviet Communism, the Second Vatican Council blowing like a wind from Heaven through the Church. Furthermore, in Pope Paul VI liberation theology had a sympathizer, a liberal Pope who recognized the plight of the poor and the radical message of the Church to them. In Latin America and beyond, Pope Paul VI appointed progressive bishops close to their people, and seemed willing to recognize and respect their role in the Church. Other clergy, already holding high office in Latin America, like Dom Hélder Câmara and Archbishop Oscar Romero, looked with a new eye at the state of things there, and were profoundly influenced by the message of liberation theology.

SUPPRESSING THE GOSPEL TO THE POOR

By the time I encountered it and was inspired by it, liberation theology was already dying. It happened quite suddenly. The movement ran into the ground – literally, because to this day there are still *comunidades de base*, and people who cherish the dream of social and economic liberation. The new Pope, John Paul II, Paul VI's successor, elected in 1978, came from a country, Poland, that had suffered grievously under Soviet Russian occupation, and whose Church had been obliged to fight a long and exhausting battle with its Communist rulers to survive at all. The culture of opposition and defiance in Poland had made it possible for the country to maintain its own fierce sense of identity, and that culture had been rooted deep in Catholicism of a devout and traditional kind.

The Pope, a man of huge courage and commitment, wanted no truck with Communism, and in that he was aided and abetted by its strategic enemy and a friend of Poland, the United States. He was supported, too, by others with selfish motives, the landowners and wealthy business-men of Latin America. New bishops were appointed to succeed those chosen by John XXIII and Paul VI, most of them of a distinctly conservative bent. Radical bishops saw their authority curbed by the Vatican, most notoriously in the case of Cardinal Arns, whose diocese of São Paulo was hollowed out, leaving him with only part of the see he had been appointed to. The scribe of liberation theology, Father Boff, was summoned to Rome by the Congregation for the Doctrine of the Faith, and ordered to be silent. So concerned were Brazil's bishops that two of them, Cardinal Arns and Cardinal Lorscheider, accompanied him to Rome in the hope of moderating the Congregation's strictures.

The new Pope was not alone in his concern about liberation theology. His hatred of Communism, and his fear that liberation theology might pave the way to a series of Cuba-like revolutions, was shared by the United States. Long before Pope John Paul II's election in 1978, the United States had been worried about left-wing political movements in Latin America, threatening the economic system in a continent with large-scale American investment, much of it by major US corporations. In 1967, an editorial in the *Wall Street Journal* described Pope Paul VI's encyclical, *Populorum Progressio*, as 'warmed-over Marxism'.[2] After the 1969 conference, 'Towards a Theology of Liberation', held in Castigny, Switzerland, alarm mounted in the United States. Some of those present felt that liberation theology had become overpoliticized, and that its protagonists tended to think in Marxist class war terms.

Later that year, Nelson Rockefeller was sent to Latin America by the new administration, that of President Richard Nixon, to observe the situation for himself. Just over a year later, the left-wing President of Chile, Salvador Allende, was overthrown by the military, with the collaboration of the United States. After the administration of President Carter, whose sentiments were less hostile, conservative American administrations resumed their campaign against liberation theology and their support for right-wing groups in Central and South America. In 1980, members of the Council for Inter-American Security (a private organization) wrote the 'Santa Fe Report' for the presidential candidate Ronald Reagan, in which it was stated that 'US foreign policy must begin to counter (not react against) liberation theology, as it is utilized in Latin America by the "liberation theology" clergy'.[3] Washington joined the Vatican in the campaign to destroy it.

So liberation theology was killed, and with it died the hopes of millions of Latin American Catholics. Certainly it could be accused of naivety. Its protagonists used Marxist language, and some were clearly attracted to Marxist ways of thinking. They should have been more conscious of the Realpolitik of their situation, especially after Allende's overthrow. They do not seem to have known much about Communism in practice, nor about the emergence in the

Soviet bloc of a new class, the *nomenklatura*, with its own privileged status and access to power. What they did know, however, was that the exploitation of landless peasants and workers by Latin America's own elites could not be squared with Christian doctrine, let alone with the teachings of Jesus Christ.

THE LEGACY OF LIBERATION THEOLOGY

In its heyday, liberation theology did influence the policies conducted by governments in Latin America. During the period from 1960 to 1980, gross domestic product per capita increased in Latin America by 75 per cent, and during the 1970s income inequality decreased, notably in Mexico, Colombia, Venezuela and Peru. Whether for reasons of fear or guilt on the part of their rulers, the poor of Latin America enjoyed their best decade. But since 1980, most of their gains have been lost, and inequality is greater than ever.

In this skewed and imperfect global market, regulation is essential to curb the abuse of power, to provide information and to lay down minimum standards, for instance for health, safety and working conditions. Markets work badly where there is no responsible government to uphold the laws that protect buyers and sellers alike. Where markets have been liberalized, sometimes much too precipitately, in societies without property laws, bankruptcy laws, contracts based on mutual consent, land laws and labour standards, there has been ruthless exploitation. The ability to coerce has been much more relevant than the rule of law.

A depressing illustration of this was Russia, where privatization in many, though not all, cases, became a licence to asset-strip. The managers of state enterprises appointed by the previous Communist regime simply took over the profitable bits and left the rest to the taxpayers. Small wonder that global capitalism has such a bad name in Russia that many of its people would gladly trade it in for a return to the drab but secure days of the old order.

WRONG PRIORITIES

Unfortunately the world's bankers and international institutions got their priorities wrong. Instead of starting, as they did, with liberalization of prices and capital, quickly followed by privatization, they should have given pride of place to building the necessary institutional and legal framework. Once that was in place, and clearly it would take time for proud countries like Russia or Indonesia to shape and 'own' such reforms, markets would have operated reasonably beneficially. Liberalization could have been staged, as the country's institutions developed the ability to cope with it. Implicit in such a gradual changeover in the case of the transition countries, Russia and Eastern Europe, would have been the maintenance of social services like public health, public transport and education, and some kind of social safety net.

THE RUSSIAN EXPERIENCE

I have worked and lectured in Russia every year for at least a couple of weeks since the Soviet Union collapsed, and I visited it on several occasions before that. The Soviet Union's public services were not quite what they purported to be. While adequate if rudimentary provision of public services was universally available in the old Soviet days, there was a hierarchy of power, and within it public provision reflected a person's status. I have stayed in former politburo hotels and travelled in former politburo trains in both Russia and Ukraine, revealing their past glory in that peculiar combination of ornate heaviness and drab similarity which characterized Soviet grandeur, crimson carpet, gold decorations and dark, gloomy furniture. I once visited a friend, Tikki Kaul, who was India's Ambassador to Moscow, a man warmly wooed by the Soviet authorities, and permitted to be one of only three top people possessed of a Zis, the most majestic car in the Russian range. When he and I arrived at one of Moscow's great onion-domed churches, doing nothing grander than sightseeing, elderly women knelt in the muddy ditches and crossed themselves, like bit players in Mussorgsky's great opera, *Boris Godunov*. I suppose they imagined my friend was either Khrushchev or Bulganin, the rulers at the time.

But what I never saw in post-war Soviet Russia, drab and gloomy though it was, were old men heavy with the medals they had won in the Great Patriotic War, the Second World War to you and me, begging for bread, and even offering their medals in exchange. What I never saw then was a peasant in a down-at-heel commuter village, weeping over his wife contorted by the agony of a heart attack, yet unable to get her to hospital because he had no money for an ambulance. The depth of Russian bitterness at what they regard as the broken promises of Western capitalism is very real, whatever cover-up the exigencies of the war against terrorism demand.

Not all the fault lay with the West. There is no tradition of civil society in Russia, and democracy has only a flimsy hold on a country where what counts is power. The oligarchs moved in swiftly behind President Yeltsin, commanding great swathes of the economy, and in particular those few parts that were profitable, mainly in the energy field. All their lives they had been taught that capitalism was an instrument of exploitation. Once it arrived in post-Soviet Russia, they seemed determined to prove their teachers right.

THE EUROPEAN WELFARE STATE

The post-war experience of Western Europe was very different. Here were highly industrialized countries traumatized by war and aware of the mistakes made by the victors after the First World War. They were societies that put a premium on security and solidarity. In the climate of mutual aid and learning fostered by the Marshall Plan, they rebuilt their institutions, invested in export industries and also in the welfare state, and returned rapidly to the levels of civilian production they had achieved before the war.

Throughout this period of reconstruction and recovery, the United States and the United Kingdom treated the European countries as equals, and listened to what they had to say. Indeed, the architects of the Marshall Plan had from the beginning assumed that the initiative would be a shared one. Ernest Bevin's rapid response in bringing together all the Western European countries to draw up their reconstruction plans, even extending the invitation to Russia and countries in her sphere of influence, showed that the concept was widely grasped. The Marshall Plan allowed countries to develop their own versions of the free market system. Western Europe's social market system, with up to 50 per cent of gross domestic product going into public services, a proportion little changed to this day, reflected the values and attitudes of most European citizens.

Europe, even after the destruction brought by the war, was both a potential competitor and a potential market for the United States. Its culture was familiar, and there were innumerable personal ties with Americans from 'the old country', whether that was Italy, Britain or Ireland.

WHO MAKES THE DECISIONS?

The story of how the countries of the Third World have been treated is sadly a very different one. The Marshall Plan embraced the countries it was intended to help as participants, fellow builders of a new Europe. The developing countries of Africa and Latin America, many of them still colonies in the 1940s and 1950s, found the post-war settlement already in place, and the decision-making dominated by the rich countries, in particular the victors of the Second World War. Thus the Security Council of the United Nations, theoretically at least the most powerful international political body, had among its members Britain and France, but not India, the world's second largest country in population terms, nor Japan, its second largest economy, nor Germany, the third largest economy. The World Bank and the International Monetary Fund, the two global economic institutions, have long danced to the tune of the US Treasury, which has the dominant voice both on appointments and on policies. The G7, on which the major Western economies and Japan are represented, and which effectively takes the most important international economic decisions, includes Japan, but excludes both China and India, the countries in which reside over a third of the human race.

At no point has there been a serious effort to reconstruct these decision-making bodies – indeed, it would require great political courage to do so. But it is hardly surprising that millions in the developing world resent the West's dominance, and the dilatory approach to change. Developing countries also understand that the global trading and financial system is rigged against them because of the power differential that exists between them and the developed world. An instructive example is the persistence of high

tariffs on agricultural goods and on textiles even after
several GATT and WTO trade rounds, the very products
where the developing world is most competitive.

KEYNES'S PROPOSAL

John Maynard Keynes, whose ideas so much influenced
the design of the post-war Bretton Woods structure,
understood the consequences of differential power unre-
lated to competitiveness – in other words, that it was an
illusion to suppose that economics could be isolated from
politics. Recognizing the weak bargaining position of the
developing countries, he proposed a fourth pillar to
Bretton Woods, in addition to the IMF, the World Bank
and the GATT. That fourth pillar would have given
bargaining strength to the primary producers of the
developing world. It was to be a buffer stock scheme
covering a range of commodities that were sold in highly
volatile markets, with prices moving across a wide range
depending on the size of the crop and on world demand for
these commodities. The volatility made it difficult for the
producers to embark on any stable savings and investment
plan. So Keynes proposed that the lurches of the market
should be ironed out, by using the buffer stock to buy when
prices were low and sell when they were high, providing
farmers with a guaranteed price. Keynes's proposal would
have complemented the other three institutions, and done
something to empower primary producers. But the weary
negotiators could not bring themselves to address the issue;
it was simply dropped.[4]

The global economic system that was challenged by
liberation theology remains in place, not much changed
since that challenge was seen off. While millions have been
taken out of poverty, especially in China and India, millions

more are poorer, in both relative and absolute terms, than they were twenty years ago. Liberation theology, however, is an idea with a long life. Its values have filtered down into the body of the Church. The 'option for the poor' influences its objectives and its actions, as many addresses by the Holy Father indicate. The recent emergence of a new political leadership in Latin America, of whom the outstanding example is Lula, the new President of Brazil, may be the first fruit of a rediscovered commitment to the dignity of the common peoples.

THE CHURCH'S OBLIGATION TO THE POOR

The Pope is well aware of this, and continues to preach against the material selfishness of the rich countries. He speaks with passion and conviction, to the rich as well as the poor, scolding the former and empathizing with the latter. His love clearly extends to them. But the 'structures of sin' remain, systems of landholding, taxation and public expenditure that consistently favour the rich.

To give credence to his words, the Pope or his successor should assemble the best economists and the best community leaders he can find to shape a market that is just, to put the weight of the Church behind those who are powerless and therefore disadvantaged and to demand of the rich a recognition of their obligations to human society. Imaginative initiatives are now being discussed: a carbon tax, a Tobin tax on short-term capital movements, an extension of debt relief, additional aid linked directly to education and public health targets in the developing world. What is lacking is the political will. Having stepped back from the radical solution proposed by liberation theology, the Church owes to its most needy children an alternative that addresses their desperation and is rooted in the teachings of the Gospel, an alternative that may not be based on a political revolution but most certainly requires a spiritual one.

NOTES

1. *Human Development Report 2002* (United Nations Development Programme, 2002), p. 195.
2. *Wall Street Journal*, 30 March 1967.
3. *A New Inter-American Policy for the Eighties* ('Santa Fe Report'), published privately, 1980. Signed by 'The Committee of Santa Fe', and authored by L. Francis (Lynn) Bouchey, Roger W. Fontaine, David C. Jordan, Lt Gen. Gordon Sumner Jr, and Lewis Tambs.
4. Robert Skidelsky, *John Maynard Keynes: Vol. 3, Fighting for Britain 1937–1946* (London: Macmillan, 2000), pp. 234–36.

Chapter 6

War and Peace

The delivery of the first four of my Erasmus lectures at Notre Dame, on which this book is based, coincided with a transforming and terrible event in American history, the attack on the World Trade Center in New York and on the Pentagon in Washington. The attacks were not only cathartic in terms of the deaths of thousands of innocent and unprepared men and women in a modern inferno, but also in terms of what they demonstrated about the motives and the capacities of their terrorist authors. The public servants of New York responded with extraordinary heroism and selflessness to the disaster. The terrorists showed masterly skill at organization and information gathering, and a dedication awesome in its disregard for human life including their own.

What have we learned from this terrible event? We have been reminded again of the moral potential of human beings, their courage and resilience, their capacity to find in themselves sources of love and the strength to endure. On the Notre Dame campus, I was profoundly aware of that in the participation of students, staff and faculty alike in the open air Mass the day after the terrorist attack, and the searching for an appropriate and moral response at the student meeting the following day. Even in the immediate aftermath of the tragedy, they, like so many other Americans, were asking themselves why this catastrophe had happened, and what should be done to ensure it never happened again. And they had absorbed its harshest and most important lesson: that the United States had ceased to enjoy the invulnerability its Great Power status had apparently conferred upon it. Indeed, that status now made America a target rather than a bastion of safety.

In the months following the catastrophe of September 11, a political response began to evolve. There were two distinct elements in that response, military and humanitarian. The military response was, at first, to direct the might of the American war machine at identifiable military targets associated with the al-Qaeda terrorist network established by Osama bin Laden, a network extending to scores of countries and communities and as yet largely undetected by the supposedly sophisticated intelligence services of the developed world. This itself suggests that there is a cultural and social gulf between the terrorists and their associates and those among whom they live and work which is unbridgeable. We neither hear them nor understand them. Their beliefs are absolute, their convictions unshakeable, and our pragmatic, relativistic, secular societies repel them. Yet even if we do not understand them we still have to try to understand those for whom they claim to act, the millions who applauded and approved what they did, who form the soil in which terrorism flourishes.

Terrorism flourishes on injustice and humiliation, and on the bitter resentments they breed. It flourishes too by exploiting people whose expectations have been raised and repeatedly frustrated. When the Cold War ended, the American interest in identifying and helping potential friends and allies was replaced by at best a benign neglect, punctuated by occasional forays against countries that produce and sell drugs, and occasional peacekeeping missions of the kind favoured by President Clinton, as much in response to domestic media opportunities as political imperatives. One day soon, we will look back and weep over the opportunities we in the West missed in this post-Cold War decade to build a stable, peaceful and just world.

In Europe, terrorism has been an enervating chronic illness in Spain and the United Kingdom, a rare but fierce fever in Germany and Italy. Neither kind has threatened the life of the state, nor been more than national in scope, apart from the funding of terrorist activities from outside, in particular from North America in the case of Northern Ireland. Senior elected politicians, however, as well as judges and military commanders, have been threatened and in some cases assassinated, alongside innocent civilians.

Because the driving force behind Spanish and Irish terrorism came from fury at historical wrongs, it is very hard to assuage or eradicate, though the passing of time and the involvement of erstwhile terrorists in constitutional political processes may moderate that sense of outrage. The absolute dedication such movements demand, a dedication that does not hesitate at the taking of innocent life, even the lives of little children, nor at one's own death, is profoundly antithetical to compromise, yet compromise is of the essence of pluralist democracy. The language of our daily transactions, economic and political language, does not reach them. Perhaps no language can. But there is some evidence that moral and spiritual language might at least reach some people aware of the suffering and injustices they themselves have borne, potential recruits to terrorist movements, and persuade them to find means other than revenge and retaliation to assuage their pain.

South Africa's Truth and Reconciliation Commission is one example, where the confessions of those implicated in

the murder and torture of many South African blacks
brought to both sides a kind of understanding and peace of
mind.[1] Another was the apology of the Pope for the evils of
the slave trade on his visit to Africa, and yet another the
prayer for forgiveness of Willy Brandt, then Chancellor of
West Germany, at the Warsaw ghetto. Dimly we are
beginning to understand that we need to grasp and
acknowledge what we have done to others before we can
conduct a useful dialogue on the construction of an
international legal and moral order. Those among us whose
countries have wielded, and often abused, their power over
others, have a special responsibility to examine our histories.
Nationally, as much as individually, none of us is blameless;
all of us need to be forgiven.

Within a few days of the attacks on New York and
Washington, President George W. Bush announced that the
United States was at war with terrorism, a phrase picked up
and proclaimed repeatedly by the media. Politically,
describing the attack as an act of war was attractive. It
had immediate resonance with the American people,
rallying them to the flag, enabling the call-up of reservists
to proceed without objection and summoning from Congress a bipartisan, patriotic response expressed in a Joint
Resolution of support. It gave the President great freedom
of action.

The War Powers Act, adopted in the two world wars,
which gave the President exceptional emergency powers,
had been repealed in 1976 by a Democratic-dominated
Congress keen to punish President Nixon for his Watergate
transgressions. But the War Power, invoked by President
Lincoln during the Civil War on the basis of combining his
position as Commander-in-Chief with his civil role, was
ready to hand for any President once war had been declared
– or, in this case, de facto declared by an act of war. While

not formally a Declaration of War, the Congressional resolution passed on 14 September 2001 would almost certainly be sufficient to satisfy the Supreme Court, should anyone question the President's use of the War Power.[2] Furthermore, the use of the term 'war' seemed to make sense. A serious and violent attack on a sovereign state, as at Pearl Harbor, is surely an act of war.

But is it? The trouble with this 'war' is that it refuses to fit into the usual definition of war as a conflict between sovereign states initiated by the attack of one on the other, or on a third party protected by a sovereign state. In a brilliant analysis published in *The New York Review of Books*,[3] Stanley Hoffmann persistently asked the question, 'Who are we fighting?' Neither Osama bin Laden nor his network of terrorists is a sovereign state. Terrorists operate outside the Westphalian structure which still conventionally defines international relations, on the basis of loyalties that are religious, ideological or cultural, but in all these instances disregard national borders. Fundamentalist Islamicists declare that their loyalty to Islam takes precedence over their loyalty to the country of which they happen to be citizens.

Trying to fit an offensive so alien to our thinking into the Westphalian order has compelled President Bush's administration to define the enemy as not just the terrorists themselves but also those states that harbour them, finance them and help them. Indeed, as the war proceeded, the overthrow of the Taliban regime in Afghanistan became a central war aim, one susceptible to being described in the familiar terminology of victory and defeat. Iraq became the second country to be so targeted. It is a sovereign state, but at the time of writing (January 2003) no links between it and al-Qaeda had been proved.

Defining terrorists as the enemy is treacherous territory, not least because every nation wants to exclude from this slippery definition those it regards as freedom fighters rather than terrorists. To avoid including the Irish Republican Army or ETA within the scope of what it is to be an enemy, phrases like 'of global reach' are employed, but if IRA activists train guerrillas in Colombia, does that pull the IRA within the definition or not? What about the vicious terrorist group that operates in the Great Lakes region of Africa without regard for national borders, the Interhamwee? Is it excluded from the definition because it is a regional terrorist group rather than a global one? Is the same true of Tamil terrorist movements operating in India as well as in Sri Lanka? And what about the Oklahoma bombers and the Unibomber, inside America itself? Should we draw a distinction between terrorist movements in countries where there is a democratic process enabling people to protest and seek redress for their grievances peacefully, compared to tyrannies where no peaceful protest is allowed?

More than being slippery, there is a momentum in the idea of 'war' that both feeds and determines the way decisions are made and who makes them that may limit both our imagination and our understanding of how to respond. Father Bryan Hehir, in his article for *America* Magazine, 'What Can Be Done? What Should Be Done',[4] warns of the dangers.

> Even if one is convinced that there must be a military dimension to an effective response to terrorism, it is better not to locate the whole effort under war ... It is better to forfeit the rhetorical bounce that comes from invoking war and define more precisely what we can and should do.

Senior members of the administration are trying to tailor the public expectations aroused by use of the word 'war' to the reality of fighting terrorism. That 'war' will be long. Victory in the conventional sense may never be attained. 'We are looking at a sustained engagement that carries no deadlines,' according to the Secretary of Defence, Donald Rumsfeld. Furthermore, 'military force will likely be one of many tools we use ... "battles" will be fought by customs officers stopping suspicious persons ... and diplomats securing co-operation against money laundering.'[5]

All of this sounds much more like the struggle against organized crime or illegal drugs than like conventional war. There are no final victories; the effort is ongoing and continuous. There are no states clearly definable as guilty or innocent, because terrorists are to be found everywhere, and there are no declarations of war. Some states will have surrendered their sovereignty to private criminal actors, as in the case of the so-called 'narco-states', or even, for a while, Russia under the oligarchs, but such a surrender is more often proof of the weakness of a state than of its complicity. In countries such as Sierra Leone, Angola or the Democratic Republic of the Congo, the governments' writ runs only over parts of the territory, usually around the capital. Guerrilla groups have seized control of the most valuable resources, in particular diamonds or gold, and the governments are powerless against them unless they can attract the help of an outside power or of the international community. Rich countries bear considerable responsibility for their plight, since all too often they condone by their inaction trading in these looted resources. Failed or collapsed states are dangerous places in which to live; the breakdown of law and order is at least as serious as its abuse.

In every state there will be some individuals or groups inclined to terrorism, domestic or international, but that will not itself make the state a terrorist one, any more than the Oklahoma City bombers so defined the United States.

Terrorism, like crime, exists everywhere, and has to be fought everywhere, because it is parasitical on civil society and will, if not contained, destroy it. I deliberately use the word 'contained' because, like crime, disease, or evil itself, I do not believe it can be wholly eradicated.

Defining the attacks on the World Trade Center and the Pentagon as crimes against humanity rather than as war would have offered immense advantages. Given the already widespread use of war terminology, members of the anti-terrorist coalition may have to introduce this concept gradually, for instance in UN Resolutions and in subsequent phases of the strategy. But this does not lessen its advantages. 'Crimes against humanity' makes the response to terrorism a global, not a national one, nor even one of a coalition of nation states. Terrorists are defined as enemies of all the citizens of an orderly and law-abiding world. There is no temptation to define them in national or religious terms. The definition, however, needs to be precise. If there is no peaceful redress for wrongs, no democratic or constitutional process that is open to him or her, then the dissident may indeed be a freedom fighter rather than a terrorist.

Second, retaliation against those who perpetrate a crime against humanity falls within the international legal order, and must therefore be measured and proportionate. As we know from the history of the last century, that is far from true of wars fought between sovereign states. Thirdly, the punishment is not 'victors' justice', but global justice, based upon the values and traditions shared between judges from different cultures holding in common respect for human life and the protection of the innocent. The proper punishment for the bin Ladens of the world is the same punishment that will, if he is found guilty, apply to Slobodan Milosevic for crimes against humanity, many of them perpetrated on

Muslims. It is important to remember that General Mladic, directly responsible to Mr Milosevic, killed some 5,000 Muslim civilians in cold blood at Srebrenica in 1996, a crime against humanity similar in scale and brutality to that of bin Laden.

Treating the attacks as crimes rather than acts of war mobilizes all those who believe in justice, human rights and the rule of law on the same side. Treating them as acts of war divides one nation from another, compelling them to take sides on the basis of national interest.

President Bush's decision to try bin Laden and his associates, if captured alive, before a military tribunal was particularly unfortunate. A military tribunal works by different rules from a civilian court, or from an international tribunal like that in the Hague now trying war crimes in the former Yugoslavia. The defendant is not free to choose his own lawyer. The rules of evidence are circumscribed. Most serious of all, the proceedings are secret. No verdict reached by such a tribunal, however carefully conducted, will be accepted by international opinion as fair. Similarly, the lengthy detention of alleged terrorists in Guantanamo Bay by the United States is completely contrary to the rule of law. Either they are prisoners of war, with rights under the Geneva Conventions, or they are alleged offenders with the right to a trial and access to lawyers. By refusing to release their names, the United States has deprived them of the rights to which every man and woman is entitled.

The great glory of democratic countries, namely the independence of the courts, the openness of the procedure and the assumption that a person is innocent until proved guilty, are being sacrificed to political expediency for reasons that are obscure and do no credit to the US administration.

It would have been easier for the United States to arraign bin Laden and his associates as perpetrators of crimes against humanity if Congress had been willing to ratify the proposal for an International Criminal Court. The treaty setting up the court had been ratified by 87 countries as of January 2003.[6] The US Congress objected on the grounds that American citizens might be brought within its jurisdiction. The American administration is now trying to conclude bilateral treaties with friendly countries under which those countries will bind themselves not to extradite any US citizen for trial by the court. If many countries enter into such agreements, the ICC will be seriously damaged. Other countries may also demand special treatment for their own citizens. Yet the United States has been compelled to recognize that it itself harboured unwittingly domestic and international terrorists too.

No instrument is more appropriate for dealing with terrorism than the ICC. The court's judges will be drawn from every country that accepts the rule of law, and will base its judgments on universally shared values and traditions, not least on the evolving doctrine of universal human rights. It is a post-Westphalian instrument, because, like the European Court of Human Rights at Strasbourg, it can override the jurisdiction of sovereign states, and that is indeed the point. Neither organized criminals nor terrorists respect borders or nationalities. In the simplest terms, good guys and bad guys are to be found in every nation. The aim must be to bring the good guys together to defeat the bad guys – or, more elegantly, to ensure that good prevails against evil.

Religious and ethical considerations become more relevant to a struggle defined in these terms, which no longer attempts to identify good and evil with particular nations or peoples. There has always been something deeply offensive about the blessing of the guns or bombs of a particular nation by men supposedly dedicated to the service of God, even more so when their commitment is to the Prince of Peace.

As the conduct of modern war has tossed aside one moral restraint after another, the identification of Christianity with any particular nation becomes perilous and hypocritical. In the First World War, young men died, some choking to death on mustard gas or blown apart by landmines. Their lives were thrown away almost casually by the military and political leaders of the time. According to contemporary reports, General Haig, Chief of the Imperial General Staff, visited in 1917, three years into the war, the devastated fields of Flanders, pitted with shell-holes. He asked his subordinates, 'Did we send men into this?' Wilfred Owen, a poet as well as a soldier, wrote their bitter elegy:

> What passing-bells for these who die as cattle?
> Only the monstrous anger of the guns.
> Only the stuttering rifles' rapid rattle
> Can patter out their hasty orisons.
> No mockeries for them from prayers or bells
> Nor any voice of mourning save the choirs, –
> The shrill, demented choirs of wailing shells;
> And bugles calling for them from sad shires.

> *'Anthem for Doomed Youth', in* Poems by
> Wilfred Owen with an Introduction by Siegfried
> Sassoon. *London: Chatto and Windus (1921)*

Yet these men were, however reluctantly, soldiers. The distinction made by the churches, and most specifically by the Vatican, between soldiers and civilians as legitimate targets of war, was largely observed on the Western Front, and elicited passionate condemnation from the other side when it was breached. Here was an assumption that certain

117

moral codes were shared. 'Poor little Belgium' stirred up fierce emotions in 1914 when rumours spread that 'the Huns' had raped Belgian women and mutilated Belgian children.

Some rules still governed warfare at the beginning of the Second World War. As a child, I used to watch dogfights between Messerschmitts and Spitfires from a trench on the Dorset downs near my school. I can still remember the victorious pilot, whether German or British, dipping his wings to the pilot who had been brought down as a mark of respect. It was said that the victor, once he was out of the area, often radioed his opponent's position to make sure that he was rescued.

Such gallantries were abandoned after the Blitz on British cities in 1940 and 1941. Both sides then embraced the doctrine of total war, to which few of the rules of war applied. Strangely enough, those that did related primarily to the armed forces, such as the Geneva Conventions on the treatment of prisoners of war and those wounded in battle. No such rules obtained in the case of civilians. The Blitz stimulated the most fearsome retaliation, obliteration bombing of German and later Japanese cities directly targeted at the civilian population in an effort to break its morale.

The Popes, from Pius XI on, repeatedly inveighed against the bombing of civilians and pleaded with the antagonists to spare the lives of mothers, children and the elderly, few of whom could properly be described as combatants. They were not heard. Perhaps one reason for Pope Pius XII's relative silence on the Holocaust was his awareness of another crime against humanity, this time by the Allies, in their relentless destruction of German cities and in the deliberate incineration of hundreds of thousands of German and Japanese civilians. No just war theory could ever encompass within its moral rules the barbarous excesses of the Allies, any more than it could the unspeakable atrocities perpetrated by the Nazi regime. In neither case could it be argued that these war crimes were essential to the conduct of the war. That war numbed the moral sense of the victors, which could not be justified by pleading the evils done by the vanquished.

The traditional distinction between combatants and non-combatants has remained in abeyance in the years since that war. In Vietnam, the Vietcong guerrillas deliberately hid among the peasants of the rural villages, and supplied their armies through neutral Cambodia. Responding, the US Air Force repeatedly bombed the villages and the Ho Chi Minh trail in Cambodia, killing thousands of civilians.

Ruthlessness about the loss of innocent life was not restricted to warfare. The history of China's Great Leap Forward and its Cultural Revolution is studded with mass killings, like those of the Soviet Union between the wars. The manifestation of extreme evil known as genocide emerged in Cambodia out of the ashes of the Vietnam War, engulfing everyone with a higher education or a knowledge of foreign languages, and leaving as its memorial neat piles of skulls.

How can any kind of moral structure be reimposed on a world so far gone in degradation? Until September 11, the Western world had retreated from responsibility, maintaining national systems of law and order as best it could, and tentatively establishing co-operative relations with other states to fight organized crime or the trade in illegal drugs, co-operation that is still at a rudimentary level. In the European Union, for instance, police forces in the fifteen member states work together to fight cross-border crime, trade in illicit drugs and trafficking in human beings, particularly children, in an organization called Europol.

There are difficult problems of accountability to the national governments and parliaments responsible for policing; Europol is the product of events, rather than of far-sighted long-term planning. As such, it is yet another example of the asymmetry between our largely national political institutions and the global challenges they have to deal with, but at least it represents a serious effort to harness governments together in a common response.

Occasionally, either because it feels threatened or because of old historical connections, a Western power or powers may intervene to stop some particularly grim atrocity, as NATO did to prevent ethnic cleansing in Kosovo, Britain in Sierra Leone and Belgium, briefly, in Rwanda. But until the September 11, 2001 terrorist attacks, there was little political will in either the United States or the European Union to take responsibility for maintaining global order. For one thing, such interventions could evoke memories of imperialism. Western governments have been almost equally reluctant to offer substantial help to the United Nations in dealing with humanitarian crises. For years, the United States failed to contribute its share of peacekeeping costs. Many of the troops that were made available for United Nations peacekeeping operations came from developing or transition countries like Bangladesh and Ukraine, and were underequipped and inadequately trained. They needed funds to turn them into a useful force. Proposals for a permanent United Nations force, or even to earmark some national units for peacekeeping duties, have so far not got off the ground, in part owing to American obstruction.

It is easy to turn one's back as long as fundamental national interests are not involved. The rich West has distanced itself from the poor, miserable populations of the Third World, other than those large enough to promise attractive potential markets, like China, or those with valuable resources. If there is to be a legal order based on consent, it must have a basis in common values. This is where the set of norms for human interaction painstakingly constructed in United Nations' treaties and protocols, and thus bearing the imprimatur of the only global political institution the world's people possess, comes into its own.

There has been no shortage of declarations, commitments and ratifications, but there has been much hypocrisy and little effective implementation. Now at last some of the instruments to enforce the norms are being put in place. Among them are the ad hoc international criminal tribunals for the former Yugoslavia and for Rwanda. Prosecutors in these tribunals have already signalled that high office, including that of head of state, will no longer protect those responsible for war crimes from prosecution. The arrest of General Pinochet in London,[7] to answer charges of torturing and killing Spanish citizens, upheld by the House of Lords, Britain's highest court,[8] was another milestone in the long march to establish an international jurisdiction for crimes against humanity, albeit that in the UK the General escaped prosecution for medical reasons, and has done so again in Chile.

INTERNATIONAL LAW: THE SANCTIONS

Economic sanctions have long been the means of punishing states that transgress international norms. Unfortunately, the sanctions often fall on the weaker and poorer members of society, as they have done in Iraq, while the elites find ways to escape their consequences. Facing international protests about the suffering and malnutrition of Iraqi children, the American and British governments never failed to mention the large quantities of whisky, cigarettes and expensive cars that continue to be imported into that country for the benefit of the military and political leaders. At last, however, sanctions are being refined to target elites rather than entire nations. Such sanctions include the confiscation of funds held in personal accounts and restrictions on travel.

Effective international action against money laundering would block the opportunity for unscrupulous elites to make themselves rich at the expense of their fellow citizens. Politicians with no sense of the public service, no commitment to the well-being of their people, use power simply to exploit the countries they control. Leaders like Mobutu of the Congo, whose lecture I once had the misfortune to chair when all my academic colleagues had fled the scene, became vastly rich by laundering the resources of the countries with whose governments they had been entrusted. General Abacha, former dictator of Nigeria, amassed millions of dollars through demanding commissions from businesses trading in that country. His extended family, like that of General Suharto, former President of Indonesia, enriched themselves at the expense of countries a third or more of whose populations live in abject poverty. President Mugabe of Zimbabwe has grossly abused his position to assist his extended family and his friends, leaving the great majority of his countrymen and women to face hunger, unemployment and despair.

But the news is not all bad. Already at the national level, legislatures and courts are becoming much readier to act; the impeachment of Señor Echeverria, former President of the Philippines, is one such example. In that case, the redoubtable Cardinal Jaime Sin played a key part in condemning the corruption surrounding the President. Citizens of developing countries are becoming aware that they cannot prosper without good government. In that, they echo the conclusions of the World Bank, painfully learned over many years.

At the international level, despite the recognition that good governance is essential to balanced and just development, there has been considerable ambivalence. Western corporations, like Western governments, have denounced corruption but done little to discourage it. Rich Western countries are now active in pursuit of the money laundering of terrorist funds, but were remarkably unconcerned about the money laundering of public funds looted from poor developing countries. These losses in some cases dwarf the humanitarian and development aid they have received. Banks, some of them with internationally recognized names, have profited from handling laundered money, and have not been assiduous in questioning where the money came from. The dangers of terrorism may persuade them to clean up their acts.

So the framework for an international legal and moral order is nearly in place, one capable of identifying terrorism as a threat to the entire international community, and able to mount a range of instruments to penalize those responsible. Nearly in place, because the United States, the only superpower, does not accept an international jurisdiction, and is still besotted by the obsolete principle of national sovereignty. The attack on the World Trade Center demonstrated that national sovereignty is ineffective against a determined global adversary. The choice of a long-term response remains open. It may be based on international law rooted in agreed norms, or it may be hegemonic, a coalition of nation states around one powerful leader, the United States.

The Vatican, given its long history of defining the morality of just wars without regard to national interests, and its global reach, has an important part to play. Its scholars and thinkers should now be working to define those global norms, based on the common heritage of humanity.

The world's governments should be working on how best to enforce these norms on tyrants and terrorists alike.

NOTES

1. Alex Boraine, *A Country Unmasked: Inside South Africa's Truth and Reconciliation Commission* (Oxford: OUP, 2001), ch. 1: 'The Road to Reconciliation'.
2. SJ.Res.23, 'Authorization for Use of Military Force', passed by the Senate on 14 September 2001.
3. Stanley Hoffmann, 'On the War', *The New York Review of Books*, 1 November 2001.
4. J. Bryan Hehir, 'What Can Be Done? What Should Be Done?', *America* Magazine, 8 October 2001.
5. Donald Rumsfeld, 'A New Kind of War', *The New York Times*, 27 September 2001.
6. The Rome Statute entered into force on 1 July 2002.
7. General Pinochet was arrested on 16 October 1998.
8. The House of Lords ruled that Pinochet was not immune from prosecution on 24 March 1999.

Chapter 7

The Four Horsemen of the Apocalypse

The Middle Ages in Europe were a time of fear and a time of guilt. Fear was pervasive – fear of war, fear of brigands, fear of the ruler, fear above all of the hellfire ordained for sinners who did not repent. For those bearing the burden of sins, the churches reminded them over and over again of the eternal penalties they were risking. The walls of mediaeval churches were adorned with murals of the Last Judgement, their tombs with horribly realistic representations of skeletons, or, even worse, mouldering bodies devoured by worms and maggots.

Mediaeval people were used to death. Most of their children died before they grew up; illnesses and injuries took a heavy toll. Dead bodies were not quickly disposed of by cremation or by well-run funeral homes. They appeared at last rites (as they still do in the world's remote places). I remember, as a teenager, attending a wake in a mining village in County Durham, with the body of the departed propped up in one corner while his friends drank to his memory.

The Lyke Wake walk in North Yorkshire runs from Helmsley to Robin Hood's Bay, over the bleak Cleveland

Hills. 'Lyke' is an Old Norse word for a dead body. Some
corpses were carried for days along the windy moors until
they reached the sea.

Some scourges, however, went beyond the everyday
burdens of life, labour and death. Many good Christians
believed these scourges to be manifestations of the wrath of
God with His feckless people. Many still do. Among the
most powerful representations of these scourges was
Albrecht Dürer's *Four Horsemen of the Apocalypse*. You may
remember seeing his drawing of those terrifying figures,
wild-eyed, ragged, with matted hair and claw-like hands,
riding their ferocious steeds. They struck terror into the
hearts of men and women. They symbolized the four worst
scourges of the human race: war, pestilence, famine and
death.

THE FIRST HORSEMAN: FAMINE

Famines still occur. Rains fail and floods destroy arable
land. Diseases may decimate herds, as foot and mouth did
last year in the United Kingdom, where four million
creatures were slaughtered and incinerated.[1] The destruction of forests in countries like Nepal and India, Brazil and
Indonesia, leads to floods and then to droughts as rainwater
and top soil together slide into the nearest river or sea, no
longer held back by trees and vegetation. I recall seeing the
Amazon like a brown stew, engulfing the fragile soil of the
rainforest after coffee had been planted where trees once
grew, on soil too thin to bear crops year after year.

But the harvests in North America and Australasia,
sustained by chemical fertilizers and high-yielding seed,
produce enough grain to meet any emergency needs. The
world's food stocks are quickly brought to bear on
threatened famine. The speedy response of international

charities, and through them of governments, usually prevents famine turning into starvation. The Nobel laureate, economist Amartya Sen, pointed out in his seminal essay *Poverty and Famines*[2] that democracies rarely experience famine. In open societies, the threat of famine becomes known, so that steps can be taken to avert famine itself.

The problem is no longer insufficient food, as it was when the old Horseman galloped across the world. It is the inability of Third World rural communities to sustain themselves, their social structures and their self-respect. Many of these communities have become global dependants, living from one handout to the next. Neither development aid policies nor the administrators of agricultural subsidies have yet seriously addressed the issue of sustainability. Translated from economic jargon, what that means is respect for the dignity of rural men and women, helping them to earn a decent living and to maintain their families. Do you recall the words of St Vincent de Paul? 'It is not enough to give a man bread. You must love him and ask his forgiveness for having to do so.'

THE SECOND HORSEMAN: PESTILENCE

The Horseman called Pestilence has changed his appearance, but has not vanished. The Western world puts its faith in science and technology to deal with the scourge of disease. Medical science – and, in particular, the establishment of the humble branch of medicine known as public health in the second half of the nineteenth century – has controlled or even eliminated some of the most fearsome diseases known to humankind, such as smallpox and leprosy, well known in the time of the historic Jesus. Antibiotics, truly miracle drugs, fight infection, and have become the doctor's answer to everything from flu to post-operative infections.

In the Western world, and among elites everywhere, the loss of a child or the death of a young person is now a rarity, a catastrophe to be specially mourned. The gravestones in nineteenth-century cemeteries tell us how common such deaths were only a century or so ago. Nineteenth-century novels describe in harrowing detail the loss of young women in childbirth, of young men from tuberculosis and the deaths of those who perished from diseases caught in exotic countries. Few children grew up to adulthood without encountering serious illness and death in their own families. The one great comfort was that death was the gateway to another, better world, where the dead would rise again, as their Redeemer had promised.

THE THIRD HORSEMAN: WAR

War, the third of the ancient Horsemen, embarrasses us because it brings death in its wake. The toll of wars has been incalculably great. The nineteenth and twentieth centuries, because of the advances in weapons technology, were hugely costly in lives. More men died in the American civil war than in all the international wars fought by the United States before and since. Western nations have now adopted military strategies that ensure wars entail few casualties for us. Our wars are sanitized. The language of our wars itself is disinfected – 'collateral damage', 'surgical strikes', 'precision bombing'. But we cannot distance ourselves altogether. Television pictures of huddled dead bodies, people shot or burned at close range, villages reduced to shards, these images haunt us. In spite of our superior knowledge and technology, the four Horsemen remain with us, in one form or another. Like our forefathers, we have little idea how to deal with them.

THE FOURTH HORSEMAN: DEATH

In the modern Western world, men and women swing uneasily between denying death and a half-belief in an afterlife. Brian Sibley, the biographer of the magical writer C. S. Lewis and his wife, Joy Davidson, used as his title a word that well describes this half-belief, *Shadowlands*.[3] The Greeks saw Hades as a land of shadows; the land of the dead who had been rowed across the Styx by Charon the oarsman. But because we value empirical fact, a shadow-land is unsatisfactory. We know almost nothing about the time after death, only a few meditations by holy men and women and a few recollections from those that passed briefly into unconsciousness on an operating table and then revived. Those recollections repeat the images of a tunnel and at the end of it a blazing light; but that is all we have to go on.

Deep in our souls we are frightened of death; partly because what lies beyond is unknown, partly because we may feel we will have to account for our lives. But even of the Judgement we are unsure. So we defy death. We use military metaphors: 'he lost his long battle with cancer'; 'she has had a heart attack'. Addressing his dying father, the Welsh poet Dylan Thomas wrote:

Do not go gentle into that good night,
Old age should burn and rave at close of day;
Rage, rage against the dying of the light.

> *Dylan Thomas, 'Do not go gentle into that good night'.*
> In Country Sleep, *New Directions (1952)*

In practice, our fear of death takes the form of delaying it for as long as possible. A huge proportion of expenditure on drugs and health care is lavished on the elderly. (In the

United States, whose infant mortality figures rate thirty-first in the world out of 173 countries,[4] 29 per cent of expenditure on health care in 2000 was spent on the last year of life, struggling against the inevitable.)[5] The quality of patients' lives in their last year or so is unlikely to be satisfactory, and so the case for euthanasia is strengthened. But there is a better answer. Hospices control pain, and help patients and their families come to terms with death. In the best-run hospices, patients are prepared for death, and meet it calmly.

When I was the MP for Crosby, I visited my local hospice on several occasions. I found it to be a happy place, illuminated by the love for his dying patients of the priest who ran it, Father Joseph, and alive with the laughter of his young assistants. I cannot help comparing it with the sullen nursing homes I have visited on both sides of the Atlantic, where frail elderly people wait apathetically to die. Our wealthy societies cannot overcome death; so instead death has been segregated, put out of sight, as far as possible forgotten about until the dead person in the funeral home has been made up to look alive before being cremated and disposed of in a sanitary urn of ashes.

THE OLD SCOURGE: THE PLAGUE

In 1346, after a generation-long financial and banking crisis, rumours reached Europe of a terrible pestilence laying waste to China. It moved with great speed, engulfing the Middle East and reaching Europe a year later. In that historical period we now think of as long before globalization, bubonic plague had travelled by way of trade. It followed the Silk Route taken by caravans of camels and horses from China to the Caucasus and the Crimea, and had thence been carried by the merchant ships of Genoa to Italy and beyond. The 'Black Death', as it came to be called, became the source of a literature of irony and despair. Petrarch, the inventor of the sonnet and one of Italy's greatest mediaeval poets, lost to the plague his beloved Laura. This is what he wrote:

> When will posterity believe that there was a time when without combustion of heaven or earth, without war or any other visible calamity, not just this or that country but almost the whole earth was left uninhabited ... empty houses, deserted cities, unkempt fields, ground crowded with corpses, everywhere a vast and dreadful silence.[6]

Among illiterate peasants, folklore about the plague developed. How many of us are aware of the irony in that otherwise charming folk song:

> Ring a ring of roses
> Pocketful of posies,
> A'choo! A'choo!
> We all fall down.

Red rings on the face were among the first signs of the plague, and posies of flowers were believed to have the power to ward it off. Death was preceded by acute fits of sneezing.

The Middle Ages looked for an explanation for the plague among divine or diabolic forces. Some held that men were being punished for the excesses and corruption of the previous glittering century, a corruption that had engulfed Church and state alike. Others found a scapegoat in the Jews, thousands of whom were put to death for their alleged part in bringing the plague to Europe. By the time the

131

plague had run its course, a third of the population of Europe was dead.

THE NEW SCOURGE: AIDS

It was six hundred years of steady advances in medical knowledge before a disease with similar lethal consequences emerged in the Western world. It is called AIDS, and it is on course to kill a third or more of the population of Central and Southern Africa, the continent where it first emerged, in the next two decades, leaving millions of children orphaned, tearing families apart and wrecking the hopes for more productive economies able to raise the living standards of Africa's people.

The probable toll in Asia and Latin America cannot be predicted, but the number of people affected by HIV, the precursor of AIDS, in these continents, in Russia and in the former Soviet states, is large and rising rapidly. Some 28 million souls have already been lost to the disease, and some 70 million have been infected with HIV,[7] though most have not yet developed AIDS.

This scourge is on the scale of the Black Death, and, like the Black Death, it is global. The scientific community knows how to mitigate the effects of HIV, though not how to cure it. But treatment is expensive, has side effects and, for much of the world's population, above all those living in Africa, is simply unaffordable. The most effective form of prevention, which is public education on the dangers of the disease and how people can protect themselves, has been undermined by cuts in school and health budgets, as governments try to claw their way out of the financial crises of recent years.

AIDS is not only a disease; it is the child of poverty. Certainly wealthy countries have suffered too. No one could deny that who has seen pictures of the demonstrations in California and elsewhere in the United States demanding more effective treatment of AIDS victims. Furthermore, in wealthy as well as poor countries, AIDS has elicited extraordinary human acts of solidarity and love from among the friends and families of victims, an unsung but impressive response. Nevertheless, AIDS is settling into the pattern of other major diseases, where, for lack of knowledge and adequate health services, the poor suffer most. Over 60 per cent of American women suffering from AIDS are African-American, as are 65 per cent of AIDS-affected children.[8] Worldwide, 90 per cent of the new cases diagnosed every day are in developing countries.[9]

AIDS has presented the Church with a painful dilemma. Experts agree that education of the public is the single most effective weapon against AIDS. Major campaigns of public education, led by the countries' most prominent political and religious leaders, have led to dramatic declines in the incidence of HIV infection in Senegal, Uganda and Thailand, to take three examples. By contrast, in South Africa, where the country's President, Thabo Mbeki, has expressed uncertainty about both the causes and the effects of AIDS, the proportion of people infected now exceeds 20 per cent, and continues to rise rapidly. Since the victims are disproportionately young, over half of them under the age of 25, South Africa's future development is jeopardized. AIDS is not only the child of poverty, it is also the father of future poverty, as it devastates the most energetic and enterprising sectors of society.

AIDS is not only the scourge of the young; even more, it is the scourge of the marginalized, those living on the edge of society. The highest levels of infection are found among drug users and prostitutes. Some will say that these pathetic dregs of humanity deserve the disease. Like their mediaeval forebears, such moralists believe AIDS is God's revenge on sin. That was not Jesus's response, as He moved among the lepers and outcasts of His own society. He understood how we humans create our own wretchedness through what are now called 'the structures of sin'. Remediable poverty is one such structure. Such is the wealth of the world that poverty is no longer inevitable.

A 'JUSTICE ISSUE'

One Catholic writer, Lisa Sowle Cahill, called AIDS a 'justice issue'.[10] It is important to try to understand what she means. AIDS clearly has its most devastating effects on those who do not know how to avoid the disease, on those who do not know how to mitigate its effects and on those who have no other means of livelihood than the work of their own hands and the exploitation of their own bodies. The educated and the comfortably off are much more likely to survive than the uneducated and the poor. Women are often innocent victims, especially if they live in patriarchal societies where married women have no rights and little influence over their husbands. So are children to whom AIDS is transmitted at birth, the saddest victims of all. For the Church to preach abstinence as the first line of defence against AIDS is simply unrealistic in such societies. The use of condoms, though contrary to traditional Church teaching, in these circumstances is a prophylactic against death, not against life. The same can be said of needle exchange for drug users.

HIV-AIDS is also a short-term threat to peace and stability. Armies, including peacekeeping forces, have a much higher incidence than the overall civil population. Ironically, peacekeepers are often associated with a sharp rise in the incidence of AIDS, as they mingle with the local population and seek out sexual partners. AIDS can even be a weapon of war, associated with systematic rape. The Warburton Report on Bosnia (1993)[11] found that the Serb army, to destroy the future local Muslim population, deliberately used rape, because raped women were regarded as unmarriageable. In some parts of Africa, intercourse with a virgin is believed to be a cure for AIDS; the consequences of that belief beggar imagination.

Apart from transmitting the disease to others, AIDS victims make heavy demands on overburdened health services and hospitals. Untreated, sufferers are unable to contribute to the local economy. Already all the gains in longevity in Africa over the past twenty years have been nullified by deaths from AIDS. Expectation of life for a newborn baby has dropped by over twenty years in sub-Saharan Africa. Hopes of economic development and a better standard of life have been devastated. The hardest blow of all to those hopes was the terrorist attack on New York and Washington. The fight against terrorism has diverted attention from the fight against AIDS, although the victims of AIDS are counted in millions.

NOTES

1. A total of 4,213,000 animals were slaughtered, including 582,000 cattle, 3,481,000 sheep and 146,000 pigs, according to the Department for Environment, Food and Rural Affairs (UK, 2003).

2. Amartya Sen, *Poverty and Famines: An Essay on Entitlement and Deprivation* (Oxford: OUP, 1981).

3. Brian Sibley, *Shadowlands: the story of C. S. Lewis and Joy Davidson* (London: Hodder & Stoughton, 1985).

4. *Human Development Report 2002* (United Nations Development Programme, 2002).

5. Jack Meyer, Sharon Silow-Carroll and Sean Sullivan,

'Critical Choices: Confronting the Cost of American Health Care' (Washington DC: National Committee for Quality Health Care, 1990), p. 52.

6. Petrarch is quoted in Hugh Trevor-Roper, *The Rise of Christian Europe* (London: Thames & Hudson, 1966), p. 165.

7. UNAIDS, the Joint United Nations Programme on HIV/AIDS, 2002.

8. Centers for Disease Control and Prevention (USA, 2002).

9. 'Facts about health', published for the World Summit on Sustainable Development, Johannesburg 2002, by the United Nations Department of Economic and Social Affairs.

10. Lisa Sowle Cahill, 'Aids, Justice, and the Common Good', in James F. Keenan, SJ (ed.), *Catholic Ethicists on HIV/AIDS Prevention* (New York: Continuum, 2000), pp. 282ff.

11. *EC Investigative Mission into the Treatment of Muslim Women in the Former Yugoslavia: Report to EC Foreign Ministers* (Warburton Report, 1993), published by WomenAid International, London.

Chapter 8

The Kingdom of God

'Man tends towards good,' wrote Pope John Paul II in his Encyclical Letter, *Centesimus Annus* (1991), 'but he is also capable of evil'. The letter celebrated the centenary of the remarkable encyclical of Pope Leo XIII, *De Rerum Novarum*, a milestone in the development of Catholic social teaching in the industrial age.

This tendency towards good can be seen everywhere in people's personal lives, and in their interaction with their local communities. As an MP, I saw over many years how men and women coped with heavy burdens, such as fragile elderly parents, handicapped children and serious illness, and, with few exceptions, demonstrated patience, understanding and endurance in doing so. I saw too the time and energy many people put into helping their local communities through a great range of voluntary activities, some associated with the churches, some not.

I never cease to wonder at the willingness of many to devote themselves to unpopular causes, such as assisting prisoners and refugees, sometimes encountering blame for doing so. All over the world there are men and women literally risking their lives to bring food and medicines to the wretched of the earth. One hears their voices from Afghanistan, Sierra Leone, the Congo, El Salvador, telling us in simple and moving terms why they are there and what they are doing. Few of them use theological language, some of them are not believers. But all of them are labourers in the vineyard, and all of them are helping to build the Kingdom.

It is easy to be pessimistic about our world. The evidence of greed and the dominance of material values is all around us. I wrote about that in the first chapter of this book. There are serious doubts about the ability of our finite and precious planet to sustain economic growth for many more years without fatal damage to the environment and its ecology. Huge inroads have already been made into the legacy human beings inherited from nature, the forests of the Amazon, the savannahs of Africa, the lakes and rivers of Central Asia.

Environmental destruction has occurred in the First World also; witness the floods that swept through Prague, Salzburg and other cherished historic towns and villages recently in Central Europe. Some parts of the environmental legacy are already past saving, including hundreds of species of insects, birds and mammals. None of us yet knows what will be the consequences of global warming, but few of us now doubt that it is real, as we read of desertification, drought and the melting of glaciers and permafrost.

But there are grounds for optimism too. The human spirit, in its tendency towards the good, has inspired hundreds of thousands of people to form voluntary organizations which today constitute a formidable political force, listened to by governments, business corporations and international institutions. Indeed, I would go further. For a long time, these established bodies tried to ignore the voluntary organizations, as an elephant ignores a gnat. So the voluntary organizations learned how to compel attention by becoming the sources of reliable and untainted information, and by attracting the interest of the public and the media.

Hesitantly, a few significant institutions began to listen to them, even to invite their views. Some corporations committed themselves to ethical investment and to codes of conduct governing how they managed their businesses. International institutions, like the World Bank and the OECD (the Organization for Economic Co-operation and Development), arranged seminars on how they had conducted their own missions. A critical and well-informed public demanded greater accountability from those who wield power in the world. The problem is the age-old one: how to make men and women see, hear and listen.

A GATED WORLD

Despite their experience of AIDS, the rich countries of the world have distanced themselves from the devastating march of the disease through large swathes of the developing world, as they have distanced themselves from poverty, hunger and ignorance. I am reminded of those gated communities in which well-off people live, cut off from the miseries and suffering of the society around them. We who are prosperous have created our own gated world. We observe in the Third World from a safe distance what we find fascinating or mysterious: African wildlife, Asian mysticism, for instance, but most of us interact very little with the people who are outside the global elite.

'Too long a sacrifice can make a stone of the heart,' wrote the great Irish poet, William Butler Yeats, in his poem 'Easter 1916'.[1] If we are not stony-hearted, we can at least turn our backs on the unbearable misery of so much of the globe. 'I can't bear to look,' we say. We walk past the homeless man in the cardboard box, telling ourselves he is probably a drug addict who has brought his plight on himself. We avert our eyes from the beggar, and close our ears to the people seeking our help.

Supposing we did look; supposing we saw not the image but the human being, suffering pain, bereavement, misery like us, but on a much greater scale. 'If you prick us, do we not bleed?' Shylock asked Portia in Shakespeare's tragedy, *The Merchant of Venice*. E. M. Forster, the author of *A Passage to India*, that luminous novel about the encounter between two very different cultures, put it in two words: 'Only connect'.

In December 2001, I heard one great lecture, and read another. Both were delivered by men who wielded considerable power. The first was the Dimbleby lecture, given by President Clinton at the invitation of the BBC.[2] It was a wonderful lecture, imaginative, empathetic, visionary. From the material of his own experience and memory, he wove a cloth of gold, a shining vision of a world of peace and prosperity which was attainable by today's leaders from today's global resources. Throughout the lecture, I was conscious of the man's love for humanity, and I am not being sarcastic. Undisciplined and promiscuous he may be, but there is a massive engine of warmth in the man.

Then I read a much more sober, academic lecture, by another powerful man, Gordon Brown, the formidably intelligent Chancellor of the Exchequer – in US terms, Secretary of the Treasury – in the United Kingdom, who has devoted much of his time to pondering how the economic inequalities of the globe can be narrowed, indeed, how extreme poverty can be abolished.[3] His vision, for all that it was painted in the monochrome pallet of economics, was a generous one. It required a greater commitment of development aid by the governments of the rich countries, an opening up of trade in products now protected or subsidized by them, a responsible partnership with the private sector and a much greater recognition by the international financial institutions of the necessity of good education and good health services as prerequisites of economic growth and development. There was even a welcome admission that the headlong rush to liberalize capital flows in the 1980s had been a mistake, overwhelming fragile and unsophisticated banking systems in the emerging market economies of East Asia and Russia.

The lecture was a blueprint for a more just world order. But it overlooked the greatest obstacle to its achievement; there was no mention in it of the probable consequences of the new plague, HIV.

THE TRAGEDY OF GOOD INTENTIONS

The President of the United States is said to be the most powerful man in the world. The Chancellor of the Exchequer is certainly one of the two most powerful men in Great Britain. No one doubts that they have the political will. But neither, despite several years in office, has been able to make a great deal of difference to the world's aching inequalities. Why?

Bill Clinton had the best of intentions. But to win the confidence of the financial markets, he appointed men who strongly upheld the so-called Washington consensus, the orthodoxy of neo-liberalism, which has never been over-concerned about the poor. Gordon Brown has pursued his own objectives more subtly, first establishing his bona fides with the financial markets, a sine qua non for a modern politician of the centre left, and only then trying to edge them towards a more far-sighted and generous perception of their own interests – truly, to use Max Weber's telling phrase, the 'boring of hard boards'.[4] It remains to be seen whether he will get anywhere, but the current absorption of the United States in its war against terrorism, almost to the exclusion of any analysis of terrorism's causes, makes the task harder. Those of us who come from countries other than the United States must somehow get across to its administration that military means will not heal the deep fractures of the world, nor reconcile the developing world to injustice.

We pray in our churches for leaders of vision and wisdom. The paradox is that, even when we have them, there seems little they can do. Power, at least in a democracy, is not like the gold ring on a circus merry-go-round, or the wizard's magic charm, something that makes all things possible. It is held in many hands, and there has to be consensus to make things happen. For them to happen to the benefit of the whole society, rather than any individual or group within it, there has to be a perception of the common good.

When I was a child, I imagined that being an MP would give me the power to bring about all kinds of good things for society. Election constituted a kind of anointing. But it was not like that. Politics indeed turned out to be the boring of hard boards. Success, such as it was, owed as much to persistence and doggedness as to inspiration. When I became a Cabinet Minister, I imagined I would have the power to do good. But what I saw as good was not identical with what others saw as good, and what I achieved was highly controversial. Some of it has been undone since. Power, I learned, was limited, transient, betraying. And it had to be that way, for nothing corrupts like unlimited power. One winter my husband and I stumbled across a ruined castle in the Atlas mountains of Morocco. The words scrawled by some unknown hand on the crumbling wall were the ancient wisdom. 'Sic transit gloria mundi,' it read. So passes the glory of the world.

THE POWER OF INDIVIDUALS

The achievements of some give the lie to those who believe individuals can change nothing. One of the most heartening experiences of my public life was the demonstration by tens of thousands of people in Birmingham to relieve the burden of debt on poor countries. The campaign was started by a small group of men and women, some associated with the churches, looking for an appropriate way to mark the millennium. It called itself Jubilee 2000, and soon became unstoppable. Thousands of people made their way to Birmingham, by bus, train and car, paying for themselves, bringing their babies and their children, to form a human chain around the city symbolizing the chain of debt.

All day long people listened to speeches, talked about strategies, discussed their objectives with strangers united only by the common cause. There were not many political leaders nor many ecclesiastical dignitaries. But certainly the Holy Spirit moved among those who came. And the campaign had an effect, for it led to an initiative to reduce the debt of the poorest countries, the so-called HIPC programme. HIPC was not generous enough and the conditions were difficult to meet, but the world had been made aware of the problem, and at least a start had been made on dealing with it.

There is now an international initiative to try to define what are the obligations of human beings to one another, to form a declaration of human obligations to match the declaration of rights. These duties are economic as well as political and moral. They spell out in secular terms what the church has been extolling for centuries, that discipleship is about service. John Fuellenbach in his book *The Kingdom of God*,[5] puts it this way: 'The second characteristic of Jesus's commandment of love is expressed through "service of neighbour". The model is Jesus Himself, who puts concern for the neighbour's well-being above everything else.'

A DECLARATION OF HUMAN OBLIGATIONS

I spent a fascinating four days in Valencia, Spain, several years ago at a meeting of people from all over the world chaired by Mr Justice Goldstone, former Chief Justice of the Supreme Court of South Africa. The declaration of Human Obligations we drew up together has had some influence on deliberations at the United Nations and in the European Union, but has not so far achieved equal status with the Declaration of Human Rights. The reason is obvious; a declaration of Human Obligations lays unequal burdens on its signatories, for the burden of obligation depends upon the capacity to bear it. But the recognition that rights must be matched by obligations moves the argument on from its source in the French Revolution to a more holistic and more religious concept of the good society.

Pope John Paul II's gathering in Assisi in 2002 with leaders of other faiths is exactly what is needed. In the past, discussions have been held between politicians and economists, but they need to be conducted in the religious and spiritual dimensions also, where secular power is not the dominant factor. Nor should secular power be the criterion for who participates in such discussions. We know already a little about the insights of tribal peoples, such as the native Americans and South America's indigenous Indians, into the relationship of man to nature. We need to approach the accumulated wisdom of peoples far removed from our own experience with due humility and openness.

The Vatican, given its long history of moral teaching and its global reach, should have a part to play in all this. Its scholars and thinkers should now be co-operating in defining these global norms, based on the world's religious and ethical traditions, and on the common heritage of humanity.

CROOKED TIMBER

From the crooked timber of humanity, no straight thing was ever made.

Immanuel Kant[6]

I am a politician, so I think in terms of institutions, laws and policies. I have set out in Chapters 5 and 6 the outline of a response to the world's challenges which reflect part of what we have learned from the teaching and example of Jesus Christ. I am well aware that even if such a system were to be constructed, everything would depend on the attitudes and objectives of the men and women who operate it. Human beings can rebel against the 'structures of sin', as the liberation theologians tried to do in Latin America, but they have to employ human beings to erect the structure that replaces them. Karl Marx believed that his utopian post-Communist society would be run by perfected human beings, but he, like Jean Jacques Rousseau and all the other political absolutists did not know how to perfect them. That is why 'no political society can ever be confused with the Kingdom of God' (John Paul II in *Centesimus Annus*).

The only lasting achievement therefore lies in changing people, and that cannot be done by coercion. They can be cowed, intimidated or killed, but not changed. What changes them, as Jesus repeatedly told us, is love. Let me offer a banal example. For a year or so, I was Minister for Prisons. My nostrils still twitch when I hear the word 'prison', because it reminds me of that peculiar mixture of smells of urine, sweat and polish I grew familiar with. Senior prison officers, unsentimental repositories of years of gritty experience, used to tell me: 'The lads are trouble until they meet a girl they really care for. Once that happens, they don't give trouble any more.'

All of us have seen members of our families and our friends transformed by love, love of a child, of a spouse, of God Himself, a force so strong that it can light up the human presence. Yet we rarely speak of its power. Our Western societies appear cynical, hard-boiled, money-driven. In truth they are famished for lack of love, and all the shopping in the world cannot make up for that.

THY KINGDOM COME

Thy Kingdom come. Do we really want it to? Christians hold conflicting images of their Redeemer. There is Christ in Majesty, King of Kings, Lord of Lords, what human beings expect of the Godhead. And there is the humble Jesus, the child born in a stable, the unknown companion of the apostles at Emmaus, the man who washed his apostles' feet. The Church has its own conflicts, on the one side the attractions of influence and power, walking with princes, on the other the example of clergy and lay people who have identified with the yearnings and the sufferings of the people of God, whatever their race or gender, as Jesus Himself did. It is those who follow and live out Christ's teachings who strengthen our faith in a time of doubt.

NOTES

1. William Butler Yeats, 'Easter 1916', as published in *The Dial*, Vol. LXIX, No. 25 (New York, November 1920).
2. Richard Dimbleby Lecture 2001, given on 14 December 2001 by Bill Clinton, entitled *The Struggle for the Soul of the 21st Century*.

3. HM Treasury, *Tackling Poverty: A Global New Deal* (London: HM Treasury, 2002).

4. 'Politics as a Vocation' (1919), from *Max Weber: Essays in Sociology*, ed. H. H. Gerth and C. Wright Mills (New York: OUP, 1946), p. 128.

5. John Fuellenbach, *The Kingdom of God* (Maryknoll: Orbis, 1995).

6. Kant wrote: 'Aus so krummem Holze, als woraus der Mensch gemacht ist, kann nichts ganz Gerades gezimmert werden.' Immanuel Kant, 'Idee zu einer allgemeinen Geschichte in weltbürgerlicher Absicht' (1784), *Gesammelte Schriften*, Vol. 8, p. 23.

Index

Note: S.W. = Shirley Williams.